Early praise for *Build Chatbot Interactions*

Effective teams automate their workflows, and chatbots are one of the best ways to capture and share repeated tasks. Daniel Pritchett is the perfect teacher to get you instantly productive creating chat-integrated automations.

➤ **Avdi Grimm**
  Head Chef, RubyTapas.com

Daniel Pritchett's *Build Chatbot Interactions* is a fantastic, comprehensive guide to getting started with programming your own Lita chatbot. It walks you through the basics of the Lita chatbot framework, how to get it up and running, and includes a wide variety of example applications. From interactions with remote APIs, to scheduled tasks, to rudimentary artificial intelligence, there are interesting and practical examples for everyone. You'll be inspired to implement your own ideas, and the book will help you figure out how. This book should be your first step after you finish the software's own documentation.

➤ **Jimmy Cuadra**
  Creator, Lita.io

Every company I have worked at has used ChatOps as a team tradition to work together and be successful. Daniel lays down the foundation for how you can get started building and deploying your first Chatbot. He then walks you through several how-to examples that explain how you can use Chatbots to manage software systems, send sms/email, schedule tasks, and much more. I recommend you get started with Chatbots today!

➤ **Tammy Bütow**
  Principal SRE, Gremlin

A delightfully comprehensive dive into the world of making chatbots. Great for hobbyists looking to pick up a new skill or professionals who want to build better tooling.

➤ **Randall Koutnik**
  Senior Software Engineer, Slack

Build Chatbot Interactions

Responsive, Intuitive Interfaces with Ruby

Daniel Pritchett

The Pragmatic Bookshelf

Raleigh, North Carolina

Many of the designations used by manufacturers and sellers to distinguish their products are claimed as trademarks. Where those designations appear in this book, and The Pragmatic Programmers, LLC was aware of a trademark claim, the designations have been printed in initial capital letters or in all capitals. The Pragmatic Starter Kit, The Pragmatic Programmer, Pragmatic Programming, Pragmatic Bookshelf, PragProg and the linking *g* device are trademarks of The Pragmatic Programmers, LLC.

Every precaution was taken in the preparation of this book. However, the publisher assumes no responsibility for errors or omissions, or for damages that may result from the use of information (including program listings) contained herein.

Our Pragmatic books, screencasts, and audio books can help you and your team create better software and have more fun. Visit us at *https://pragprog.com*.

The team that produced this book includes:

Publisher: Andy Hunt
VP of Operations: Janet Furlow
Managing Editor: Susan Conant
Development Editor: Tammy Coron
Copy Editor: Paula Robertson
Indexing: Potomac Indexing, LLC
Layout: Gilson Graphics

For sales, volume licensing, and support, please contact *support@pragprog.com*.

For international rights, please contact *rights@pragprog.com*.

ISBN-13: 978-1-68050-632-7
Book version: P1.0—June 2019

Contents

Preface

Welcome to *Build Chatbot Interactions*.

Chat is a compelling and accessible medium, and it's everywhere—mobile phones, tablets, computers, you name it. It keeps us connected, and it's endlessly programmable. There's room for creativity, convenience, wonder, and excitement.

Chat includes dialog like:

- "Hi, how have you been?"
- "Are you free for lunch tomorrow?"
- "Show me another funny picture."
- "Find me some tickets to NYC for next Friday."

A *chatbot* is a program that exists where users already hang out—in chat rooms and messaging programs. Thanks to chatbots, users don't have to scroll through endless pages or links looking for what they want. Instead, chatbots offer smaller, back-and-forth interactions with a conversational style. You ask the chatbot a question, and it gives you an answer. This type of interaction is more personalized and provides the user with immediate, focused assistance.

The classic chatbot style is a single user in a chat room that has a specific name, like Eliza, Bob, or Computer. The bot you'll work with in this book is named "Lita" after the Ruby-based chatbot building framework you'll learn to use. This particular user is available 24/7 to answer certain types of questions and perform *known tasks*. These known tasks are referred to as *chatbot skills* and are the primary focus of this book.

A chatbot skill is a bit of code that responds to a specific question with a relevant answer. Here's an example:

> You: *Lita, show me a picture of my dog*
>
> The bot: *Ok, here's one! http://instagram.com/fake-photo-url.jpg*

If you break it down into a few components, it looks something like this:

- The end user supplies a specific plain-text question or command.
- The bot performs a relevant programmable action to fulfill the end user's wish.
- The bot responds in plain text.

In this book, you'll walk through the design and implementation of your own chatbot skills, and you'll deploy these skills as *always-online services* that you can use as you see fit.

Who Is This Book For?

This book is for anyone who's interested in ideas and examples to help build useful and entertaining chatbot interactions. While all of the examples in this book are in Ruby, an experienced programmer can translate them into any language.

This book is equal parts entertainment, instruction, and inspiration. If you're not a confident programmer, don't worry. All of the code examples are tested and executable—you can download, run, and expand on these examples later as needed.

What's in This Book?

This book has several sections. First, you'll set up your own chatbot using the Lita framework in Ruby. From there, you'll create a few sample bot interactions to get your feet wet. After that, you'll deploy your new chatbot to the internet so you can share it with friends. Along the way, you'll learn how to integrate with external APIs, send messages, and perform sysadmin tasks, and how to connect to common "Internet of Things" devices.

What You Need

You'll need a computer that can run Ruby 2.0 or newer. You'll also need an internet connection so you can deploy your bots.

What you won't need, however, is lots of money—you can work through most of the examples using free tools. Several others can be pulled off with free trials and simulators from popular services.

The chatbot skills in this book were developed on a MacBook and the live production bot was published to Linux servers. The Lita framework should work pretty well for development in Windows, but you'll have an easier time on Linux, macOS, or even the Windows Subsystem for Linux. At the time of this writing, Ruby and Lita do work on Windows, but many common Ruby gems won't work out-of-the-box unless you're on a Unix-based system.

Why Lita and Ruby?

I selected Lita for this book, because its design and licensing make it ideal for learning, training, and sharing. The project itself is open source, so you'll be using it freely.

The way Lita provides chat skills—which it calls *handlers*—is great for readability, testability, and modularity. As you work through this book, you are going to make individual Lita skills that are publishable as well-tested, standalone Ruby gems.

Online Resources

The code referenced in this book is available on the book's website.[1] You're encouraged to download and run the examples, especially if you get stuck or want to see the finished product.

Acknowledgements

First and foremost, I'd like to thank my family for supporting and encouraging me through the process of writing this book. My wife, Chandler, and my daughter, Leila, have kept me excited and engaged throughout the process. This book would be nothing without the services of my trusty development editor, Tammy Coron. Thank you for your friendly and firm introduction to the world of print publishing. I am supremely grateful to this book's technical review team: John Dugan, Lance Hilliard, Mark Locklear, and Josh Nichols. Warm thanks to the fellow creators who provided pre-release review quotes and support: Avdi Grimm, Tammy Bütow, Randall Koutnik, Amir Shevat, Jimmy Cuadra, and Ryan Bigg.

There are far too many people to thank than I could ever remember, but here's an attempt: The volunteer staffs of PyTennessee, Southeast Ruby, and Southeast Solidus conferences for giving me a chance to share chatbot fun with fellow developers. The creators of Hubot for bringing me my first truly exciting chat development experience. Jimmy Cuadra for creating the Lita framework that made so many of this book's examples possible. John Dugan and Tim Lowrimore for guiding me through my first exciting years as a Rubyist. Brian Hogan for many efforts shepherding me through publishing

---

1. http://pragprog.com/titles/dpchat

and career journeys. The Clear Function team for supporting and encouraging me in the earliest days of this project. My beta readers and technical reviewers. George Spake for demonstrating the magic of a public chatbot through his first tentative contributions. The dozens of Twitch viewers who cheered me on during live book coding sessions, including—but certainly not limited to—Matt McCullar, John Hall, Jason Myers, Jessica Biggs, and Roger MacIsaac. Without every one of you, this book wouldn't have been possible.

## CHAPTER 1

Your First Lita Bot

Before you can start building fun and functional chatbot skills, you need a bot. In this chapter, you'll get your Lita bot up and running, and that starts with Ruby. But first, you need to determine on which operating system your bot will run: Linux, macOS, or Windows.

Here's the hard truth: The Ruby ecosystem's collective energies are aimed at Linux first, macOS second, and Windows a distant third. Linux is preferred because so many developers build their production software using Ruby and host on a commodity cloud-based infrastructure. Because Linux has been swallowing up that market for decades now, most Ruby gems you'll use are most likely to work on Linux and least likely to work on Windows. macOS usually works, largely because MacBooks are a popular development platform for professional Rubyists.

Don't worry, Windows users, there's still good news: Microsoft added a Linux compatibility layer to Windows 10 called the Windows Subsystem for Linux[1] (WSL), which provides a Linux command-line experience for Windows 10 users. The WSL provides an impressive, feature-rich, high-compatibility Linux experience at the command line inside of a Windows environment. For the purposes of this book, let's assume you're using desktop Linux, macOS, or the WSL.

Linux and WSL users

The examples in this book are written and tested against Ubuntu, so you're better off starting there if you don't have a strong need to use a different flavor of Linux. Once you have installed Ubuntu-on-WSL and can open a terminal, you're ready to proceed to the next section and follow instructions marked "Linux/WSL."

---

1. https://docs.microsoft.com/en-us/windows/wsl/install-win10

Install Ruby

For Linux and WSL users, you can get Ruby by running sudo apt-get install ruby. For macOS users, you need to install the Homebrew[2] package manager first. After that, you can get Ruby by running brew install ruby.

Before moving on, confirm your installed versions of Ruby, gem, and Bundler:

```
~ ruby --version
ruby 2.5.1p57 (2018-03-29 revision 63029) [x86_64-linux]
~ gem --version
2.7.6
~ bundle --version
Bundler version 1.16.2
```

If you have Ruby 2.2 or newer, a working copy of gem, and Bundler, you're ready to go. You need both gem and Bundler to install Lita and its Ruby dependencies. If you don't have Bundler, you need to fetch it: gem install bundler.

It's time to install the non-Ruby dependencies that provide low-level functionality for some of the Ruby libraries (gems) Lita uses.

Install Shared Libraries and Redis

Ruby is great for chatbot work because it's a powerful and dynamic language. The downside of this flexibility is that Ruby isn't as fast as some other, less malleable languages. This means that certain repetitive tasks—like crunching HTML or compressing files—are better when delegated to non-Ruby code with Ruby serving as an orchestration layer. This code is commonly available in the form of shared libraries. You'll install the libraries directly onto your host machine outside of the regular RubyGems install process.

Shared libraries are typically written in a high-speed, statically typed, compiled language like C and provided for any other local programs—such as Lita—to build against. In this section, you'll install the dependencies directly onto your development machine. Ruby uses these libraries when compiling the relevant gems that need them. An example is the Nokogiri gem; it relies on the libxml2 C library to do its heavy lifting.

Next, you'll run through the command line scripts for installing the external dependencies Lita requires.

---

2.   https://brew.sh/

> \\//
> ౨ʃ   **Joe asks:**
>
> # How do I know when I need a shared library?
>
> Ruby gems manage their external dependencies at gem install time using the extconf.rb file. If you fail to install a required gem and see the message, "extconf.rb failed," head to Stack Overflow and search for packages you might be missing. For example, enter "nokogiri osx extconf" to locate missing packages for nokogiri. You can also read the extconf.rb file to see whether anything jumps out at you.

Linux / WSL

On Linux or WSL, use these commands to install the external dependencies:

```
sudo apt-get update && \
  # the compilers you'll need to bake in external library support
        apt-get install -y build-essential && \

  # a local redis datastore to provide persistence for Lita
        apt-get install -y redis-server && \

# some of the most common external libraries needed by popular RubyGems
sudo apt-get install -y patch zlib1g-dev liblzma-dev libssl-dev
```

You now have the compilers and external dependencies needed to build some common Ruby gems, like Nokogiri. You also installed Redis, which is a primary dependency for Lita.

MacOS

On macOS, use these commands to install the external dependencies:

```
# set the stage with compilers and external dependencies
xcode-select --install
```

```
# a local redis datastore to provide persistence for Lita
brew install redis
```

You now have the compilers and external dependencies to build some common Ruby gems, like nokogiri. You also installed Redis, which is a primary dependency for Lita.

Use Redis as Lita's "Brain"

Redis is a hugely popular open-source data store that provides fast key-value store functionality. Lita requires Redis as a means of storing information between chatbot interactions. Later in the book, you'll tell Lita to "Do this thing for me in five minutes," and Lita will store the task description in Redis to be retrieved and revisited later.

After you install Redis, you need to confirm it's working properly. Linux and macOS machines will likely have the Redis server running in the background as soon as the install finishes; but for WSL, you need to open a separate console tab and manually start the Redis server with redis-server.

For general Redis debugging and exploration, the redis-cli executable is installed when you install Redis. Here's a quick run-through of the basics:

```
~ redis-cli
127.0.0.1:6379> set lita "my chatbot"
OK
127.0.0.1:6379> get lita
"my chatbot"
127.0.0.1:6379> del lita
(integer) 1
127.0.0.1:6379> get lita
(nil)
```

There are a few things to note about the listing above:

- Redis is available on localhost (127.0.0.1) at port 6379 by default.

- The set command allows you to write a value and a key for later retrieval. In this example, "my chatbot" is the value for the key "lita."

- The get command tells you what, if anything, is stored at a given key.

- del removes (or deletes) the value from a given key.

For more information on Redis, view the official Redis documentation.[3]

Install the Lita Gem

The stage is set, and you're ready to install Lita. For the rest of this chapter, you'll use the same instructions whether you're on Linux, macOS, or the WSL. Start by installing the Lita gem:

```
# Install the Lita gem and its bot generator
~ gem install lita
Successfully installed lita-4.7.1
Parsing documentation for lita-4.7.1
Installing ri documentation for lita-4.7.1
Done installing documentation for lita after 0 seconds
1 gem installed

~ lita --version
4.7.1
```

---

3.   https://redis.io/documentation

If all went well, your local RubyGems installer fetched the Lita gem from rubygems.org and installed it onto your machine. You're ready to generate a Lita bot.

Generate a New Lita Bot

Before you can start using your Lita bot, you first have to create it. Issue the following command:

```
# create a new bot at ./mybot
~ lita new mybot
      create  mybot
      create  mybot/Gemfile
      create  mybot/lita_config.rb
```

The 'lita' Command

Like many gems, Lita provides a command line executable named lita. In this chapter, you use the lita command to create your new Lita bot. In future chapters, you'll use the lita command to create Lita-compatible modules called "handlers" and "extensions." These provide new functionality to a Lita bot; in this book, you'll spend most of your time working with handlers and extensions.

With this lita command, you create a new bot in a local folder named mybot. The initial Lita bot has only two files: the Gemfile and the lita_config.rb. From here, you can build out everything you need for a functioning chatbot.

Now, enter the newly created mybot folder and install Lita's base set of dependencies:

```
~ cd mybot

# install all Lita gem dependencies from ./mybot/Gemfile
~/mybot bundle
Fetching gem metadata from https://rubygems.org/.........
Fetching gem metadata from https://rubygems.org/.
Resolving dependencies...
Using bundler 1.16.2
Using concurrent-ruby 1.0.5
Using multipart-post 2.0.0
Fetching faraday 0.15.3
Installing faraday 0.15.3
Using rack 1.6.10
Using url_mount 0.2.1
Using http_router 0.11.2
Fetching i18n 1.1.1
Installing i18n 1.1.1
Using ice_nine 0.11.2
```

```
Using multi_json 1.13.1
Fetching puma 3.12.0
Installing puma 3.12.0 with native extensions
Using rb-readline 0.5.5
Fetching redis 4.0.3
Installing redis 4.0.3
Using redis-namespace 1.6.0
Using thor 0.20.0
Using lita 4.7.1
Bundle complete! 1 Gemfile dependency, 16 gems now installed.
Use `bundle info [gemname]` to see where a bundled gem is installed.
~/mybot
```

If you're not used to working with Ruby, this is a good time to stop and read through the bundle output so you can get a feel for how package management is handled:

- Bundler searches the central rubygems.org repository for each of the gems named in your Gemfile.

- Bundler resolves the various gem version requirements specified in your Gemfile against each other and attempts to find a matching set of gem versions on RubyGems.

- Bundler downloads or installs all of the gems you need.

- Certain low-level gems, puma for example, have to do some compiling in the background to bake in the shared libraries discussed previously.

- Bundler provides the bundle info command to allow you to further inspect a newly installed gem. At some point, you may also want to look up bundle show and bundle open.

Test the Bot Locally

Your Lita bot is installed but not started. To spin it up, invoke a lita command from within your bot's root directory:

```
$ lita
Type "exit" or "quit" to end the session.
Lita >
```

There's Lita—ready and waiting for your command. Ask your bot for help:

```
Lita > lita help
Lita: help - Lists help information for terms and command the robot will
  respond to.
Lita: help COMMAND - Lists help information for terms or commands that begin
  with COMMAND.
```

```
Lita: info - Replies with the current version of Lita.
Lita: users find SEARCH_TERM - Find a Lita user by ID, name, or mention name.
Lita >
```

Here, you have the results of a lita help command: The bot loops over all of the registered abilities or skills it knows and returns a one-line primer on how to invoke them.

Now, try lita info:

```
Lita > lita info
Lita 4.7.1 - https://www.lita.io/
Redis 4.0.9 - Memory used: 821.62K
Lita >
```

This is your second Lita skill invocation. Lita responds with the version information and the amount of memory Lita is consuming in Redis. Note that the normal interaction with Lita involves you addressing the bot by name, similar to how you'd interact with Siri or Alexa.

Wrap-up

In this chapter, you learned how to create your own Lita chatbot on Linux, macOS, and the Windows Subsystem for Linux. You learned about external dependencies for some heavy-duty Ruby gems, and you explored the core of Lita's text-based interface. You're ready to start building your own textual interactions using Lita as your canvas.

In the next chapter, you'll make your own Lita skill. It'll be a purposefully simple skill, good for easing you into the next layer of owning and operating a chatbot.

Challenges

At the end of each chapter, you'll find a series of challenges that present opportunities for you to expand on that chapter's themes and techniques. Your first challenge: Basic exploration of your new Lita bot.

- Lita's help command offers you several useful housekeeping and information tools. Try lita help and read over the list. Be sure to check out lita info and lita users.

- Your newly generated lita_config.rb file offers several customization options for your Lita bot. To get a feel for what sorts of common tweaks Lita operators need, skim over the comments in that file.

- At the top of your lita_config.rb file, you'll see a config.robot.name = "Lita" line. Try changing that name from "Lita" to something more meaningful to you and your bot's intended community. A bot's got personality. Personality goes a long way.

## CHAPTER 2

Your First Lita Skill

In this chapter, you'll build your first chatbot skill—a skill that doubles a given number. By building this simple skill, you'll become familiar with the critical components and processes involved in developing and publishing chatbot skills. As you work through this chapter, you'll gain a deeper understanding of how skills work, and by the end, you'll be able to build your own chatbot skills.

Here's an overview of what you will do:

- Write a route for matching specific user messages.
- Write code for responding to that route with something useful.
- Write RSpec tests to confirm that your skill works as intended.
- Set up a release pipeline so you can deploy your code to RubyGems.
- Set up public code hosting at GitHub and continuous build testing with Travis CI.

You won't, however, put your single-skill Lita bot online, at least not yet—you'll take care of that in the next chapter. But first, you need to create a skill.

Generate an Empty Skill

Before you can implement your "doubler" skill—which is at its core a Ruby one-liner—you'll need to tell Lita to create a new handler module to store your code. To create a new skill, run `bundle exec lita handler doubler` at your console. This command will create a new `lita-doubler` directory with all the Ruby files required to build your first Lita skill. All you'll need to do is fill in a few of the newly created files.

For your first skill, agree to all of the optional prompts by entering "yes." These options help you build in some quality control with your Lita skills. It's especially important to type "yes" when prompted, "Do you want to test your plugin on Travis CI?" as you'll use this later.

When prompted for a GitHub username, enter your username. If you don't have a GitHub account, you can sign up for a free one at github.com.

```
lita-doubler/examples/001_generate_skill.session
$ lita handler doubler

Do you want to test your plugin on Travis CI?
  ("yes" or "no", default is "no") yes
Do you want to generate code coverage information with SimpleCov
  and Coveralls.io? ("yes" or "no", default is "no") yes
If your plugin's Git repository will be hosted on GitHub, build status
and code coverage badges can be automatically added to your README.
Would you like to add these badges?
  ("yes" or "no", default is "no") yes
What is your GitHub username? dpritchett
      create  lita-doubler/lib/lita/handlers/doubler.rb
      create  lita-doubler/lib/lita-doubler.rb
      create  lita-doubler/spec/lita/handlers/doubler_spec.rb
      create  lita-doubler/spec/spec_helper.rb
      create  lita-doubler/locales/en.yml
      create  lita-doubler/templates/.gitkeep
      create  lita-doubler/Gemfile
      create  lita-doubler/lita-doubler.gemspec
      create  lita-doubler/.gitignore
      create  lita-doubler/.travis.yml
      create  lita-doubler/Rakefile
      create  lita-doubler/README.md
If you plan to release this plugin as open source software, consider
  adding a LICENSE file to the root of the repository.
Common open source software licenses can be found
  at http://choosealicense.com/.
Remember, for badges to be displayed in your plugin's README, you must
  host your project on GitHub. Additionally, you will need to configure
  the project on Travis CI and Coveralls.io.
```

If everything goes well, you'll end up with a lot of files in the newly created lita-doubler folder. Here are some that are worthy of a closer look:

- README.md is the gem's welcoming area and the first thing people see when they look you up on GitHub. Use the Markdown language to format an accessible Introduction and Getting Started guide.

- lib/lita/handlers/doubler.rb contains the core implementation code for the Lita skill you're about to write.

- spec/lita/handlers/doubler_spec.rb contains an empty test harness for automatically verifying the new Lita skill works as intended.

- .travis.yml is a default configuration for a free online build server. Later, you'll set this up to automatically test each new release of your Lita skill as you push it out to GitHub.

- lita-doubler.gemspec specifies all of the important metadata you'll need to make your Lita skill publishable as a RubyGem.

Complete the Gemspec

The new Lita doubler skill is nearly ready to run. However, you still need to complete the gemspec file. Replace the "TODO" blocks with a proper description, summary, and home page link. If a project doesn't have its own website, it's common to point to a public repository, like GitHub. The following shows a completed gemspec file.

```
lita-doubler/lita-doubler.gemspec
Gem::Specification.new do |spec|
  spec.name          = "lita-doubler"
  spec.version       = "0.1.2"
  spec.authors       = ["Daniel J. Pritchett"]
  spec.email         = ["dpritchett@gmail.com"]
  spec.description   = "Doubles numbers - simple demo skill"
  spec.summary       = "Doubles numbers - simple demo skill"
  spec.homepage      = "https://github.com/dpritchett/lita-doubler"
  spec.license       = "MIT"
  spec.metadata      = { "lita_plugin_type" => "handler" }

  spec.files         = `git ls-files`.split($/)
  spec.executables   = spec.files.grep(%r{^bin/}) { |f| File.basename(f) }
  spec.test_files    = spec.files.grep(%r{^(test|spec|features)/})
  spec.require_paths = ["lib"]

  spec.add_runtime_dependency "lita", ">= 4.7"

  spec.add_development_dependency "bundler", "~> 1.3"
  spec.add_development_dependency "pry-byebug"
  spec.add_development_dependency "rake"
  spec.add_development_dependency "rack-test"
  spec.add_development_dependency "rspec", ">= 3.0.0"
end
```

This gemspec provides RubyGems enough information to know:

- Where to host this gem: https://rubygems.org/gems/lita-doubler
- How to list it in the directory
- Where the source code is stored should users want to view it

A quick word about the host location and gem names. To publish skills on RubyGems, the gem name must be unique. Meaning, you can't publish another copy of lita-doubler. However, the process described in this chapter works for any new Lita gems you create—provided their names are unique. If you're determined to publish this gem immediately, you need to change the spec.name line:

```
                           # this one might not be taken yet!
spec.name                  = "lita-doubler-but-with-a-unique-name"
```

Quick test your new skill

Now that your gemspec is complete, it's time to test your skill to make sure everything's working. First, run bundle install to install the gem's prerequisites, which are listed at the bottom of the gemspec. When that's done, you can start the gem with bundle exec lita.

The following log is from a smoke test session on the new lita-doubler gem.

```
lita-doubler/examples/003_first_run.session
$ vi lita-doubler.gemspec
$ bundle
fatal: Not a git repository (or any of the parent directories): .git
Fetching gem metadata from https://rubygems.org/........
Fetching gem metadata from https://rubygems.org/.
Resolving dependencies...

... skipping gem install manifest for brevity ...

Bundle complete! 8 Gemfile dependencies, 40 gems now installed.
Use `bundle info [gemname]` to see where a bundled gem is installed.
$ bundle exec lita
fatal: Not a git repository (or any of the parent directories): .git
Type "exit" or "quit" to end the session.
Lita > lita help
Lita: help
  - Lists help information for terms and command the robot will respond to.
Lita: help COMMAND
  - Lists help information for terms or commands that begin with COMMAND.
Lita: info - Replies with the current version of Lita.
Lita: users find SEARCH_TERM - Find a Lita user by ID, name, or mention name.
Lita >
```

Because this is a new, empty Lita skill, it doesn't do much. However, you can still test whether or not a skill is switched on by using lita help, as shown in the log.

Teach Lita when to respond with a route

As you saw in the log, the Lita bot powering your new skill can already respond to the help command. Now, you just need to teach it how to respond to skill-specific commands. You can make this happen with a route directive:

```
lita-doubler/lib/lita/handlers/doubler.rb
route(
  /^double\s+(\d+)$/i,
  :respond_with_double,
  command: true,
  help: { 'double N' => 'prints N + N' }
)
```

If you've built web applications, Lita routing likely looks familiar.

Validate your first route with a unit test

Writing bot skills can get frustrating when your handler doesn't acknowledge the expected trigger words. You can avoid this by writing route tests.

The following are some RSpec tests using a Lita-specific expected.to route syntax. You can test both the positive "responds when expected to respond" case, as well as the negative "does not respond when input doesn't quite match the specified route" case. Negative tests help construct a mental model of how a specific piece of code is expected to behave. With smaller skills like the doubler, this isn't too much of an issue. However, as you create more complex skills, negative tests will come in handy.

```
lita-doubler/spec/lita/handlers/doubler_spec.rb
describe 'routing' do
  # allow extra whitespace
  it { is_expected.to route('Lita double 2') }
  it { is_expected.to route('Lita double    22') }
  # allow mixed casing
  it { is_expected.to route('Lita doUble 4') }

  # ignore numbers that don't look like integers
  it { is_expected.to_not route('Lita double two') }
  it { is_expected.to_not route('Lita double 1e4') }
end
```

Complete Your Skill and Write Some Unit Tests

Your Lita skill was created with a placeholder where you can drop in the necessary Ruby code to double a number. It's time to fill that in so Lita can start doubling numbers on demand.

The following code provides the core functionality to double a number. Type the code inside the lib/lita/handlers/doubler.rb file.

```
lita-doubler/lib/lita/handlers/doubler.rb
def double_number(n)
  n + n
end
```

Testing the :double_number method requires a simple RSpec test. The RSpec idioms used within the test are:

- A describe block—an RSpec idiom for grouping a specific context inside of a larger test suite, such as a single method under test.

- A let call. This one exposes a variable n that can be used by any tests inside the current block—your describe.

- A single test defined with the it keyword. If this test fails, the error report includes the test description and the bad output so you can debug and correct it.

- An expect call. Here, you're asserting that x equals y. If x doesn't equal y, RSpec throws an error and tells you exactly where it was when the test failed, along with the values of x and y. This should be enough for you to start a bug hunt to correct a broken method.

To confirm that the tests work, run them again by typing rake test.

lita-doubler/spec/lita/handlers/doubler_spec.rb
```ruby
describe ':double_number' do
  let(:n) { rand(1..100) }

  it 'returns double the input' do
    actual = subject.double_number n
    expected = n * 2

    expect(actual).to eq(expected)
  end
end
```

Earlier in this chapter, the "double N" route explicitly mentioned a :respond_with_double method. It's good practice to build the methods that handle the routing separately from the implementation of the functionality you're providing. This makes testing and refactoring cleaner for you, the author.

Look at the :respond_with_double method. Its response input parameter is a Lita object representing the chat message that triggered the call to lita-doubler. Here, the handler method calls the doubler method, stores the result, and sends it back to the user message object with a response.reply call.

lita-doubler/lib/lita/handlers/doubler.rb
```ruby
def respond_with_double(response)
  # Read up on the Ruby MatchData class for more options
  n = response.match_data.captures.first
  n = Integer(n)

  response.reply "#{n} + #{n} = #{double_number n}"
end
```

Lita's test helpers provide a :send_message method that lets you send a user-like message to Lita, such as "lita double 2." It then checks a replies object to see whether Lita responded as expected.

lita-doubler/spec/lita/handlers/doubler_spec.rb
```
it 'doubles numbers when asked to' do
  send_message 'Lita double 2'
  expect(replies.last).to eq('2 + 2 = 4')
end
```

Publish Your Skill for Others as a Ruby Gem

When your skill is ready, you may want to share it with others. To properly deploy your gem and share it with others, you'll perform the following steps:

- Create a new GitHub repository to match your gem's name—in this case, lita-doubler.

- Register the remote repository URL with your local git repository via git remote add.

- Push your skill's source code to GitHub with git push.

- Register your newly populated repository with Travis CI for automatic test builds.

- Publish your working gem to RubyGems with rake release.

Before publication, you need to get the code on GitHub so you can hook up the other services.

Set up a repository for the gem on GitHub

By now, you should already have a GitHub account. After you're logged in, you can create a new repository for your project. It's best to give it a name that matches the gem name—in this case, lita-doubler, as shown in the figure on page 16.

After the new repository is created, you need to register the remote server as a "git remote" destination using the following commands. Be sure to use your account name and not mine (dpritchett)—if you don't use yours, these commands will fail.

```
$ git remote add origin git@github.com:dpritchett/lita-doubler.git
```

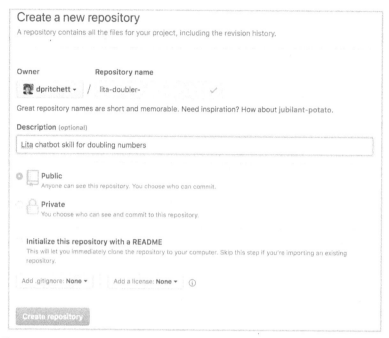

When the remote repository is open, you can commit your work and push it to GitHub.

```
lita-doubler/examples/002_push_to_github.session
$ git add .
$ git commit -m "Add everything for first push to GitHub"
[master (root-commit) 3cd0382] Add everything for first push to GitHub
 22 files changed, 298 insertions(+)

 create mode 100644 .travis.yml
 create mode 100644 Gemfile
 create mode 100644 Gemfile.lock
 create mode 100644 LICENSE
 create mode 100644 README.md
 create mode 100644 Rakefile

... skipping list of files for brevity ...

 create mode 100644 spec/lita/handlers/doubler_spec.rb
 create mode 100644 spec/spec_helper.rb
$ git push
Counting objects: 33, done.
Delta compression using up to 8 threads.
Compressing objects: 100% (28/28), done.
Writing objects: 100% (33/33), 18.01 KiB | 4.50 MiB/s, done.
Total 33 (delta 4), reused 0 (delta 0)
remote: Resolving deltas: 100% (4/4), done.
To github.com:dpritchett/lita-doubler.git
 * [new branch]      master -> master
```

With the code successfully pushed to GitHub, you're ready to set up continuous integration on Travis CI.

Set up a build server on Travis CI

When you generated the lita-doubler gem at the start of this chapter, you were instructed to type "yes" for the prompt, "Do you want to test your plugin on Travis CI?" Saying yes to this gives you access to the Travis CI build configuration file.

The .travis.yml file informs Travis of the following things:

- Which Ruby versions to use to test your code.

- Which supplemental services are required for the build to run—in this case, just Redis.

- Which command kicks off a build or test run. For this gem, the build command is rspec spec, just like you ran locally.

```
lita-doubler/.travis.yml
language: ruby
rvm:
  - 2.2.6
  - 2.3.3
install:
  - bundle install
services:
  - redis-server
script: rspec spec
```

To enable builds on a new repository, you need to sync your GitHub profile with Travis as shown in the figure on page 18 . You shouldn't need to change this file to make the build work, but you will need to deploy your code to GitHub. When that's done, you'll need to log in to Travis to set up the build. For example, if your personal GitHub account is dpritchett;, after you push your gem to GitHub, it shows up at https://github.com/dpritchett/lita-doubler.

Continuous Integration Services

Continuous integration services, such as Travis CI, help you and your Lita skills' users build confidence in the robustness of your work. Travis is a good choice because it's free for open-source projects. Use the MIT license (by default), if you want your skills to be easily consumable and freely re-shareable by other Lita users. Other options where you should be able to get a Lita build script going include: Codeship, CircleCI, Jenkins, or even Heroku's built-in CI service.

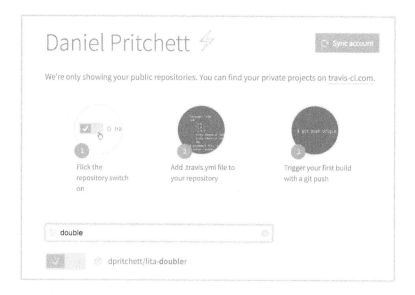

Publish the skill to RubyGems.org

If your Lita skill runs locally, has working tests, a GitHub home, and a CI build that verified that each new push works, then you're ready to push up the skill as a Ruby gem. If you don't already have a RubyGems account, you'll need to create one at Rubygems.org. When created, log into the account.

When you're ready to deploy, type rake release, and watch it go:

- A new git tag is applied to the latest commit in your repository. This matches the spec.version listed in your gemspec file and defaults to "0.1.0."

- The current tagged commit of your repository is pushed to GitHub.

- GitHub creates a "release" of your project named "0.1.0." This provides a central location for anyone who needs to download or review a specific historical version of your code.

- Rake builds your working gem as a .gem file: lita-doubler-0.1.0.gem. Gemfiles themselves are tar archives—a Unix-oriented file format that compresses this directory, and everything in it, into a single, compressed file.

- Rake creates the lita-doubler gem on RubyGems, if it's not there already.

- Rake uploads the newly created .gem file to RubyGems so others can download it on demand.

Don't forget, your push will be rejected if you kept the name lita-doubler, because there's already a gem by that name. You can try renaming the gem in the gemspec, or you can wait until you have a unique gem to publish (Lita quadrupler maybe?). If you do end up publishing a straight clone of lita-doubler, after you've finished this walkthrough, you may want to delete it to minimize clutter for RubyGems users.

Add your published gem to your bot's gemfile

Now that your skill is published to RubyGems, you can add it to the Lita bot you created in the previous chapter. Open your bot's gemfile and add a line that looks like this:

```
gem 'lita-doubler'
```

Run bundle install, and the doubler gem will be installed and ready the next time you run bundle exec lita.

Wrap-up

In this chapter, you learned several important techniques to help you grow your chatbot. You built a practical chatbot skill and tested it using lita handler. You also set up a solid release toolchain with GitHub, Travis, and RubyGems.

In the next chapter, you'll publish your new Lita bot to Heroku, a low-cost platform that's a good fit for small Ruby tools like Lita. With Heroku, your bot can listen 24/7 in a public chat channel of your choice, such as a Slack room.

Challenges

- You've made your first simplified Lita skill to double numbers. Try making another one! Maybe it could answer a common question. Maybe it could take some words as input and uppercase them or reverse them. Ruby's String library[1] is your friend here.

- This chapter showed you how to publish your first skill to RubyGems. A ton of Lita-related gems already exist on RubyGems. Search for "lita" on rubygems.org and browse through some of the biggest hits to fill your brain up with inspiration for future Lita successes.

- Redis is a key dependency of Lita's. While you won't need to mess with it directly until later in the book, why not open up the official Introduction to Redis[2] to familiarize yourself with some of its uses?

---

1. https://ruby-doc.org/core-2.5.0/String.html
2. https://redis.io/topics/introduction

## CHAPTER 3

Deploy Your Lita Bot to Heroku

Now that your Lita bot is working on your machine, you undoubtedly want to show off your bot as quickly as possible. One way to deploy your bot is using the Heroku platform; this chapter walks you through that process.

> ## Heroku Platform
>
> Heroku is a freemium Platform as a Service (PaaS) web application host. While traditional web apps might be served from a physical closet server running Linux or a $5/month Linux VM running on Amazon, Heroku provides a more streamlined experience. With Heroku, you 'git push' a Ruby repository to their servers, they install your dependencies and fire it up, and then they snapshot the result. This snapshot works a lot like a Docker container: it can be restarted nearly instantly, and Heroku allows you to jump from 1 to 5 instances of your finished application and back down to 1 if load requires.
>
> While the price and scalability are particularly nice for business uses, the key element of the Heroku experience for educational purposes is that there are simply fewer moving parts than a full-blown Linux installation. Aside from uploading the app code and configuring a few environment variables, you won't need to concern yourself with much.

You'll also learn how to use Lita adapters—gems that let Lita bots log on to public chat networks like Slack or IRC.

In learning the basics, you'll start to get a handle on the twelve-factor app[1] philosophy. These principles help guide application developers from the single-app, single-server model to a more cloud-friendly, decentralized design.

As you work through this chapter, you'll get used to twelve-factor concepts like these:

---

1. https://12factor.net/

- Logs go to STDOUT instead of a named file. This helps when your app doesn't actually live on a single, specific machine day-to-day or when it's on more than one machine. Don't worry, those STDOUT logs are still captured by logger services and streamed to a central location for you to review and search at your leisure.

- Frequently-changed or sensitive application configuration is managed by operating system environment variables. This gives you a way to reconfigure something like a password without having to rebuild and redeploy your app.

- External dependencies use consistent interfaces whether they're local or remote. A local datastore used in development can be connected to with the same network-based mechanism as a cloud-hosted datastore used in production.

If a *simple deployment with less flexibility than your own Linux box* doesn't sound like your cup of tea, there's a chapter about deploying to a traditional Linux server: Chapter 4, Deploy Lita on Your Linux Server, on page 35.

Prepare a Heroku Home for Your Bot

Before you begin, you need a Heroku account.

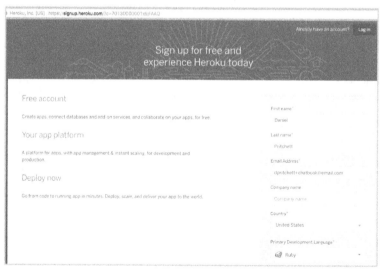

To sign up for a free account, go to Heroku.com and provide your name and email address. When prompted to pick a language, choose Ruby.

Once you're logged in, Heroku redirects you to their first-time Ruby user docs.[2] The *How Heroku Works* section provides some information about how Heroku differs from traditional self-hosted web servers. Feel free to study this guide; it's handy if you haven't used web servers before.

Install the Heroku client

Self-guided Heroku learners are likely to start with the built-in Heroku dashboard. It provides a nice visual representation of your app, its history, and the computing resources available to you. There are also mobile clients, like Nezumi, that leverage the Heroku API to start, stop, and scale your applications.

For this book, you're going to stick with the command-line heroku tool, since it's easier to follow on the written page. You can get the setup instructions[3] from the Heroku website.

On a Mac, you can use the Homebrew package manager[4] to get Heroku installed. If you don't have Homebrew, you need to install it first. Once you've got it, run a brew install heroku. When the client is installed, log in:

```
>>> heroku login
    Enter your Heroku credentials:
    Email: dpritchett@gmail.com
    Password: ************************
    Two-factor code: ******
    Logged in as dpritchett@gmail.com
```

In this example, you may notice that my Heroku account is protected by a two-factor authentication[5] code. You don't need to add that to your account yet, unless you're feeling security conscious about your Heroku apps.

Create the Heroku app

Now that you're logged in to the Heroku CLI tool, you're going to push through the setup process by trial and error. While there's a quicker way to get things working, it's best to get some experience with common mistakes and solutions so you can help yourself later on.

---

2. https://devcenter.heroku.com/categories/ruby
3. https://devcenter.heroku.com/articles/heroku-cli#download-and-install
4. https://brew.sh/
5. https://en.wikipedia.org/wiki/Multi-factor_authentication

Here's the overall plan. You'll:

- Create the heroku app.
- Layer into the app some Heroku and Slack config.
- git push the app to Heroku.
- Step through some Heroku-specific debugging and cleanup.
- Test the bot in a Slack channel.

With the heroku client installed and you logged in, it's time to create a new Heroku app with heroku create. Be sure to run this from within your chatbot's root folder—the same folder that contains lita_config.rb, your gemfile, and most importantly, your .git folder, which contains your bot's version history.

```
>>> heroku create
Creating app... done, ⬡ desolate-temple-13621
    https://desolate-temple-13621.herokuapp.com/
    | https://git.heroku.com/desolate-temple-13621.git
```

The preceding snippet shows the output of Heroku's create command. In this example, a new Heroku app was created with an auto-generated name, "desolate temple 13621."

Each app comes with its own URL at a herokuapp.com subdomain. It also comes with a similarly named git repository at git.heroku.com. The Heroku tool automatically adds your app's git repository as a git remote destination. This means you can start pushing code as soon as you're ready, using the git push heroku master command.

To confirm the new heroku git destination is in place, run git remote --verbose:

```
>>> git remote --verbose
heroku   https://git.heroku.com/desolate-temple-13621.git (fetch)
heroku   https://git.heroku.com/desolate-temple-13621.git (push)
origin   git@github.com:dpritchett/ruby-bookbot.git (fetch)
origin   git@github.com:dpritchett/ruby-bookbot.git (push)
```

You can see that heroku has been added as one of your named remote git repositories. Push your latest code to this remote repository whenever you're ready.

Prepare your bot for Heroku

You're not quite ready for the first push to Heroku. Heroku needs to know which shell command to run when it's time to kick off your bot. You've been using bundle exec lita to run the bot locally, and that's just what you want Heroku to do.

In your bot's root directory, create a new one-line file named Procfile:

```
>>> cat Procfile
web: bundle exec lita
```

The one-line Procfile tells Heroku that it can run the web component of your app on demand using the bundle exec lita command. Procfiles can declare more than one process type.

In larger Rails apps, it's common to see a web type that starts with bundle exec rails and another worker process type such as bundle exec sidekiq to manage a companion background job process. You won't need those for this project, but if you want to simulate the *multiple related Ruby processes coordinated by a single tool* style of Procfile work, there's a gem for you called foreman.[6]

Foreman provides a command-line interface to stop and start your named process types with intentions like *start two web processes and one worker process*. Again, you can safely gloss over this part and just know that Heroku is going to automatically detect and start Lita as a web-type process thanks to your one-line Procfile.

Push your bot to Heroku

One of Heroku's best features is the deploy via git push. If your app's files are laid out in a way Heroku recognizes, it'll try to deploy the app to the web as soon as you git push code to Heroku. Let's add some Slack-specific config to the Lita repository and then give the deployment a try.

While your initial work with Lita has been completely local to your development machine, public deployments require a Lita adapter to connect them to a chat gateway. In this case, you're going to help your bot log in to a Slack[7] community and interact with its users. This requires the addition of a Slack adapter gem for Lita, as well as some Slack-specific configuration, like an API key.

First, add this section to lita_config.rb:

```
# The adapter you want to connect with. Make sure you've added the
# appropriate gem to the Gemfile.

# heroku uses a RACK_ENV of 'production' by default
if ENV['RACK_ENV'] == 'production'
  config.robot.adapter = :slack
  config.redis[:url] = ENV.fetch('REDIS_URL')
else
  config.robot.adapter = :shell
end

# slack adapter demands a value even in dev when we aren't using it...
config.adapters.slack.token = ENV.fetch('SLACK_TOKEN', '')
```

---

6. https://github.com/ddollar/foreman
7. https://slack.com/

Then, add the lita-slack gem to your Gemfile:

```
gem 'lita-slack'
```

With your Lita bot's Slack adapter installed and configured, it's time to commit these changes to your git repository (git commit -am "add Slack adapter and config") and push them up to Heroku to see whether they work (git push heroku master).

```
>>> git push heroku master
Counting objects: 143, done.
Delta compression using up to 8 threads.
Compressing objects: 100% (122/122), done.
Writing objects: 100% (143/143), 62.79 KiB | 0 bytes/s, done.
Total 143 (delta 53), reused 0 (delta 0)
remote: Compressing source files... done.
remote: Building source:
remote:
remote: -----> Ruby app detected
remote: -----> Compiling Ruby/Rack
remote: -----> Using Ruby version: ruby-2.3.1
remote: -----> Installing dependencies using bundler 1.15.1
remote:        Running: bundle install
    --without development:test --path vendor/bundle
    --binstubs vendor/bundle/bin -j4 --deployment
remote:        Fetching gem metadata from https://rubygems.org/........
remote:        Fetching version metadata from https://rubygems.org/.
remote:        Fetching multipart-post 2.0.0
remote:        Fetching rack 1.6.5
... lots more bundle install happens here, snipped for brevity
remote: -----> Detecting rake tasks
remote:        Could not detect rake tasks
remote:        ensure you can run `$ bundle exec rake -P` against your app
remote:        and using the production group of your Gemfile.
remote:        bash: vendor/ruby-2.3.1/bin/rake:
    /app/vendor/ruby-2.3.1/bin/ruby:
    bad interpreter: No such file or directory
remote:
remote: -----> Discovering process types
remote:        Procfile declares types      -> web
remote:        Default types for buildpack -> console, rake
remote:
remote: -----> Compressing...
remote:        Done: 21.9M
remote: -----> Launching...
remote:        Released v4
remote:        https://desolate-temple-13621.herokuapp.com/
                 deployed to Heroku
remote:
remote: Verifying deploy... done.
To https://git.heroku.com/desolate-temple-13621.git
 * [new branch]      master -> master >>>
```

It looks like the app pushed—but if you click the link to your new app (desolate-temple-13621 in the example above), you see an error page.

Your first Heroku error

To see what's gone wrong on its maiden voyage and to figure out why Heroku wasn't able to start your bot, check the app's logs.

To view the logs, use the heroku logs command.

```
>>> heroku logs
2017-07-09T21:57:27.992354+00:00 app[api]:
    Enable Logplex by user dpritchett@gmail.com
2017-07-09T21:57:27.640110+00:00 app[api]:
    Initial release by user dpritchett@gmail.com
2017-07-09T21:57:27.992354+00:00 app[api]:
    Release v2 created by user dpritchett@gmail.com
2017-07-09T21:57:27.640110+00:00 app[api]:
    Release v1 created by user dpritchett@gmail.com
2017-07-09T21:57:39.000000+00:00 app[api]:
    Build started by user dpritchett@gmail.com
2017-07-09T21:58:09.601037+00:00 app[api]:
    Release v3 created by user dpritchett@gmail.com
2017-07-09T21:58:09.601037+00:00 app[api]:
    Set LANG, RACK_ENV config vars by
    user dpritchett@gmail.com
2017-07-09T21:58:09.971463+00:00 app[api]:
    Scaled to console@0:Free rake@0:Free web@1:Free by user
        dpritchett@gmail.com
2017-07-09T21:58:09.956564+00:00 app[api]:
    Release v4 created by user dpritchett@gmail.com
2017-07-09T21:58:09.956564+00:00 app[api]:
    Deploy 931dc07b by user dpritchett@gmail.com
2017-07-09T21:57:39.000000+00:00 app[api]:
    Build succeeded
2017-07-09T21:58:12.631552+00:00 heroku[web.1]:
    Starting process with command `bundle exec lita`
2017-07-09T21:58:14.969277+00:00 app[web.1]: [2017-07-09 21:58:14 UTC]
    FATAL: Lita configuration file could not be processed.
    The exception was:
```

```
2017-07-09T21:58:14.969298+00:00 app[web.1]:
    key not found: "REDIS_URL"
2017-07-09T21:58:14.969299+00:00 app[web.1]:
    Full backtrace:
2017-07-09T21:58:14.969299+00:00 app[web.1]:
    /app/lita_config.rb:23:in `fetch'
2017-07-09T21:58:14.969300+00:00 app[web.1]:
    /app/lita_config.rb:23:in `block in <top (required)>'
```

At the tail end of that log, you see a Ruby stack trace. It appears that Lita tried to boot but blew up with a key not found: "REDIS_URL" error. This happened because you used that ENV.fetch command in lita_config.rb.

When Ruby tried to fetch a key named REDIS_URL from the operating system's list of environment variables on Heroku, it didn't find anything. Fetch's default behavior is to fail immediately with a straightforward error message. This is a common pattern for configuring Ruby apps—if you know up front that you'll *always* need a specific configuration item set before you can boot, you may as well fail immediately if you can't find it. That's the case here: Lita insists on having access to Redis. Let's see about getting Redis set up on Heroku.

Add-ons and Heroku's Elements Marketplace

Heroku has an add-ons marketplace[8] with a handful of first-party add-ons (datastores, simple scheduled tasks) and a host of third-party tools. These add-ons provide Heroku app operators an extremely low-friction means to add common supporting software to their web applications. Where a traditional web hosting setup might expect you to operate your own MySQL or Postgres database, Heroku makes such things a click away with the add-on marketplace. Each add-on can be selected from a menu and added directly to your app, usually with little to no custom code required. Most of the add-ons have tiered pricing, and many of them have a free hobby tier. That's the case with Heroku's own Redis option. Let's turn it on.

```
>>> heroku addons:create heroku-redis:hobby-dev
Creating heroku-redis:hobby-dev on ⬡ desolate-temple-13621... free
Your add-on should be available in a few minutes.
! WARNING: Data stored in hobby plans on Heroku Redis are not persisted.
redis-dimensional-44686 is being created in the background.
    The app will restart when complete...
Use heroku addons:info redis-dimensional-44686 to check creation progress
Use heroku addons:docs heroku-redis to view documentation
```

---

8. https://elements.heroku.com/addons

This adds the lowest (free) tier of the heroku-redis add-on to this Heroku app. By default, this add-on sets a REDIS_URL environment variable for the app that will give Lita the connection string it needs to find the free Redis instance:

```
>>> heroku config
=== desolate-temple-13621 Config Vars
LANG:        en_US.UTF-8
RACK_ENV:    production
REDIS_URL:   redis://h:redacted@ec2-redacted.compute-1.amazonaws.com:19359
```

Now that Redis is wired up, check those Lita logs again.

```
2017-07-10T02:09:18.579091+00:00 heroku[web.1]: State changed
    from down to starting
2017-07-10T02:09:20.399986+00:00 heroku[web.1]: Starting process with
    command `bundle exec lita`
2017-07-10T02:09:24.051341+00:00 heroku[web.1]: State changed
    from starting to up
```

You should see a log without any errors waiting for you to interact with Lita.

Connect your bot to Slack

Now that your Lita bot builds and runs on Heroku, it's time to connect it to a Slack group.

Slack

Slack is a popular chat platform that provides groups of people with a communication center. Users log on to Slack from phones, web browsers, and desktop clients. Once logged on, they can send messages to shared channels or direct to other users. Slack supports file uploads, inline display of images, and video. Most importantly, at least for this book, Slack makes the integration of external services, like chatbots, easy enough for end users. It's common to see Slack groups with multiple bots; some are single-purpose utility bots, and others are more general-purpose like your Lita bot.

To get your Lita bot on Slack, you need a target group. I created a new one named, "chatbot book fans." You may either create a new group at Slack.com or use an existing group you've already joined.

Once you're logged in to Slack, open the apps page at your-group-here.slack/com/apps. In the search box, type "Lita" and click through to the page to add a new Lita bot.

Click *Add Configuration* to set up your Lita bot. Specify a user name for the bot and click *Add Lita Integration*. This redirects to a page with Lita setup instructions. Here, you're told to add lita-slack to your gemfile and lita_config.rb file. You get a new Slack API token that you're told to drop into your lita_config.rb. You can do it that way for now, but long-term, it's probably better to hide it behind a Heroku environment variable. Copy and paste the API key from your browser into a console like so:

heroku config:set SLACK_API_KEY="key-goes-here"

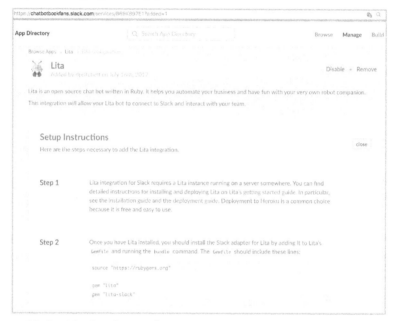

Time to add the Slack adapter for Lita to your gemfile:

gem 'lita-slack'

In lita_config.rb, you can reference the SLACK_API_KEY environment variable and only try to connect to slack when you're running a production environment.

```
Lita.configure do |config|
    if ENV.fetch('RACK_ENV', 'development') == 'production' do
        config.robot.adapter = :slack
        config.adapters.slack.token = ENV.fetch('SLACK_API_KEY', '')
    else
        # don't bother with Slack on your dev machine
        config.robot.adapter = :shell
    end
end
```

Back at your Slack integration setup page, click *Save Integration*, and then you're good to deploy.

With these additions to your Lita config file, you need to save your changes to your git repository again (git commit -am 'added slack adapter'), and then push them up to Heroku to be built and deployed (git deploy heroku master).

If you want to simulate production locally—say, your Heroku app is broken and you're having trouble debugging remotely—you can 'force-set1 the relevant environment variables at runtime, and your bot will try to log into Slack:

env RACK_ENV=production SLACK_API_KEY='your-key-goes-here' bundle exec lita.

Talk to your bot inside Slack

Now, you can go to Slack and invite your bot by name to whichever channel you choose (/invite @bookbot brings "Bookbot" to your current channel). To test the bot, speak to it in your channel. Saying @bookbot double 2 ought to reward you with the familiar 2 + 2 = 4 response from Chapter 2, Your First Lita Skill, on page 9 as shown in the following image. If you skipped that chapter, you can still add lita-doubler to your Gemfile and redeploy the bot.

Logs and your bot's responses

I can tell you from painful experience that incomplete bot skills often fail to respond at all when there's a bug in your route or in your handler code. In fact, I had that problem while writing this chapter. You don't have to relive that struggle for very long though, because Lita's built-in logging can be configured to tell you what skills, if any, each incoming chat message matches. To do this, you change Lita's log level from its default of *info* to the super-verbose *debug*.

When working with a single-machine Lita setup like your development environment, you can easily adjust your log level in lita_config.rb. On a cloud deployment like Heroku, you're much better off injecting frequently changed configuration elements using environment variables. This means you won't have to re-commit and re-deploy your codebase every single time you need to change a log level, an API key, or some other runtime concern.

It's time to dig deeper into configuring environment variables with Heroku. You already instructed your bot that its Redis server URL can be found in the SLACK_API_KEY environment variable. Later, you'll tell the bot which API token to use when connecting to Slack. Right now you need to see about setting the log level to be more verbose. Lita's documentation[9] suggests that log levels are adjusted with a config.robot.log_level setting.

First, add the environment variable log level setting to lita_config.rb:

```
config.robot.log_level = ENV.fetch('LOG_LEVEL', 'info').to_sym
```

Then, commit and deploy the change. Note that you default to info if the environment doesn't have a log level variable stored.

Finally, set the LOG_LEVEL environment variable on Heroku:

```
>>> heroku config:set 'LOG_LEVEL'='debug'
```

Whenever you update an environment variable via heroku config, all of your app's *dynos* (Heroku-speak for containers running one of your app's processes) are immediately restarted with the new values applied. No re-deploy or rebuild necessary. Let's hit the log again and see what you get from log level debug.

```
2017-07-10T00:59:40.027547+00:00 app[web.1]: [2017-07-10 00:59:40 UTC]
    DEBUG: desktop_notification event received from Slack and will be ignored.
2017-07-10T00:59:47.639682+00:00 app[web.1]: [2017-07-10 00:59:47 UTC]
    DEBUG: user_typing event received from Slack and will be ignored.
2017-07-10T00:59:51.808922+00:00 app[web.1]: [2017-07-10 00:59:51 UTC]
    DEBUG: user_typing event received from Slack and will be ignored.
2017-07-10T00:59:52.788186+00:00 app[web.1]: [2017-07-10 00:59:52 UTC]
    DEBUG: Dispatching message to Lita from U04RAL55Q.
2017-07-10T00:59:52.788469+00:00 app[web.1]: [2017-07-10 00:59:52 UTC]
    DEBUG: Dispatching message to Lita::Handlers::Doubler#double.
```

The verbose logs above show all of the information you'll need for tracing unexpected message matching behavior. The *event received and will be ignored* lines are a hint that the Slack API is sending more information than the Lita Slack adapter cares to respond to. Lita doesn't need to know whether another

---

9. https://docs.lita.io/getting-started/configuration/

user is in the process of typing a new message. The *dispatching message from U04RAL55Q* line hints that Lita and Slack have a means of tracking individual users with unique IDs. The final line is what you came for: *dispatching message to Handlers::Doubler.* Lita correctly identified the `double 2` command and routed it to the Doubler handler. When no handler routes match a message Lita receives, you see a similar log message.

Extra Heroku add-ons to consider

Sometimes, you'll want to debug something that happened to one of your apps in the context of *what was going on with this app when I wasn't looking 18 hours ago?* For those cases, I strongly suggest that you set up the Papertrail add-on.[10] This saves your logs to a web service that indexes them for fast searching after the fact. You can also set up alerts for when certain messages come through your log in a specified period—say frequent timeouts to your Redis service or your email provider.

Finally, look at the Heroku Scheduler.[11] You'll work with this one in a later chapter about scheduling Lita actions to run at specific times. Since the primary use case of a Lita bot is *person types a message and Lita responds more or less immediately*, you'll need to get creative if you want Lita to do specific things at specific times without visible user input. One use could be a timed reminder message; another might be some under-the-hood scheduled housekeeping of bot internals that doesn't need to wait for a user to remember to kick it off—think "Lita, clean your room."

Wrap-up

Congratulations, your Lita bot works locally and now it works on Heroku. With any luck, your fellow Slack users are captivated with their new bot friend, and you made several critical accomplishments in this chapter:

- Your bot can be up 24/7 and talk to people other than you. You will need to enter a billing credit card number on the Heroku site to keep the app running 24/7, but at current pricing levels you can keep a single app up without incurring fees.

- You have successfully deployed a Ruby app to Heroku.

---

10. https://elements.heroku.com/addons/papertrail
11. https://elements.heroku.com/addons/scheduler

- You know how to adjust Lita's runtime configuration using environment variables, saving you the trouble of re-committing and re-deploying, unless you're changing bot functionality.

- You've seen the Heroku marketplace and started thinking about supplemental services to keep your bot running smoothly.

The next chapter complements this one by showing you how to deploy your freshly production-readied Lita bot to a self-managed Linux server. By targeting a low-cost virtual private server (VPS), you'll have more control and more flexibility. While I'm personally happy to keep most of my apps on a PaaS like Heroku, there are times when it's nice unquestionably to run your own bot on your own server.

Challenges

- Heroku's pricing model means you may find yourself needing to tweak the size and number of your "dynos" before the end of your first month running Lita. To prepare yourself for this possibility, check out the documentation on dynos.[12]

- Next, browse the Heroku Elements Marketplace[13] to see some of the more popular Heroku add-ons and "buttons." The add-ons are third-party software that complements many Heroku use cases (primarily web applications, but maybe also chatbots). The buttons are one-click installers that allow others to instantly set up their own copy of a published program on Heroku. You could even set up a Heroku button for your own Lita bot that others can click to install.

- Heroku maintains a comprehensive set of documentation about running all sorts of applications on their platform. Take a look at Heroku's Ruby Support center[14] to survey potential roadblocks and pitfalls you'll need to work around as your Lita bot matures.

---

12. https://www.heroku.com/dynos
13. https://elements.heroku.com/
14. https://devcenter.heroku.com/categories/ruby-support

## CHAPTER 4

Deploy Lita on Your Linux Server

In the previous chapter, you explored hosting your Lita bot on Heroku, a paid software hosting platform. In this chapter, you'll look at an alternative solution that gives you a more generic deployment path (in case Heroku doesn't fit your needs): Hosting Lita on a commodity Linux server that you control. To make this work, you'll use a few common Linux administrative tools:

- An SSH connection to communicate with the server.

- The secure copy protocol (SCP) for uploading files to the remote server.

- Basic shell scripts to execute the commands required to get your bot set up for its first run.

- Docker containers to package your bot so you can send a working version from your machine to any other machine that wants to run it.

- A Makefile to script some administrative tasks surrounding the Docker container that packages your bot.

- A crontab file to manage a regular schedule to update and restart your bot.

An experienced Linux administrator may choose to forego using Docker in favor of directly installing Ruby and managing the Lita process using upstart or a similar tool. This chapter opts for the Docker-based process for two reasons: Installing and managing Ruby daemons on a Linux server can be hard for newer users, and this intro to Dockerizing Lita may be helpful for readers looking to deploy a chatbot on a container-based platform like Kubernetes.

Before you dive into all of this Linux goodness, you need to set up a Linux server. For this, you'll use a DigitalOcean droplet—what they call their virtual private servers—as your Linux server, because they offer a smooth onboarding experience for hobbyists.

Create a Cloud Virtual Machine

Registration on DigitalOcean[1] requires an email address. You won't need to supply a credit card right away—thanks to the introductory credits you receive—but if you plan to use more than that, you'll need to upgrade. The cost to operate a Lita-sized DigitalOcean droplet is about $5/month.

DigitalOcean provides a prebuilt Linux image, highlighted in the following screenshot, that runs Docker out of the box:

Once you're registered, you can create a droplet. The easiest way is to click through on *Create Droplets* and then open the *One-click apps* tab. Here, you see a *Docker* option, which creates an Ubuntu Linux server with Docker pre-installed. If this option is not available, select the latest Ubuntu, and install Docker using the instructions located at Docker.com.[2] To confirm that Docker works, run docker run hello-world on the server:

```
deploy-via-docker/examples/000-hello-docker.session
$ docker run hello-world
Unable to find image 'hello-world:latest' locally
latest: Pulling from library/hello-world
9bb5a5d4561a: Pull complete
Digest: sha256:f5233545e43561214ca4891fd1157e1c3c563316ed8e237750
Status: Downloaded newer image for hello-world:latest

Hello from Docker!
This message shows that your installation appears to be working correctly.
```

With Docker installed, you're ready for the next step. If you had trouble logging in, proceed to the next section, and then return here.

Upload your SSH key to DigitalOcean

The bootstrapping scripts you're about to run on your new DigitalOcean droplet require you to authenticate multiple times to install Docker and Lita

---

1.   https://www.digitalocean.com
2.   https://docs.docker.com/install

onto your virtual machine. Although you can enter your password each time, you're better off setting up an SSH key pair and adding it to your DigitalOcean droplet at build time. You also need to set up an SSH agent on your local machine. GitHub has some excellent documentation[3] for setting up an SSH key pair and an agent if you aren't already running one.

Joe asks:

What's an SSH key and why do I want one?

Secure Shell (SSH) key pairs are text files your computer can generate that allow you to authenticate yourself securely to other computers. The pair of files consists of a private key and a public key. Your computer uses the private key to sign work and make connections. Other computers use the public key to confirm that the bearer of a signed connection attempt is in possession of its corresponding private key.

After you create your key pair, you typically upload your public key to a server that you've logged into manually and that you plan to connect to in the future. The next time you connect, your computer can offer up the, "I have a private key here, would you like to see whether it matches any of your trusted public keys?" option, instead of a manual password-protected login.

SSH key pairs are commonly used to streamline remote access to servers including Linux hosts and code management infrastructures like GitHub.

You can add your public SSH key to DigitalOcean, so the system can add it to your new server. This saves you from having to log in at every step throughout the chapter.

Review and Run the Bootstrap Script

This single-pass installer uses a collection of setup scripts to get Lita running on Docker:

- The entry point is bootstrap_server.sh. You'll run this locally to connect to your remote server through SSH, upload files the server needs, and kick off some installers.

---

3.   https://help.github.com/articles/generating-a-new-ssh-key-and-adding-it-to-the-ssh-agent/

- The install_dependencies.sh file gets uploaded to your remote server. When it's run on the remote machine, it installs some operating system packages (Redis and make), runs your Makefile, and then installs a crontab.

- The Makefile handles the day-to-day work of starting, stopping, and updating the Docker container that runs your Lita daemon. It runs initially from the "install dependencies" script and again on a schedule via cron.

- Finally, the lita_crontab file contains a one-line schedule command that allows Ubuntu to download and run the latest version of your published Lita container periodically.

Bootstrap the server

The first script you need to run is bootstrap_server.sh. Create it using this sample:

```
deploy-via-docker/bootstrap_server.sh
#!/usr/bin/env sh

echo "** Bootstrapping lita on docker **"

echo "** Preparing to Connect **"
read -p 'What is your Droplet host name or IP address? ' DROPLET_HOST

# paste in your slack token interactively here
read -p 'What is your Slack token? ' SLACK_TOKEN
echo $SLACK_TOKEN > ./slack_token_tmp.txt

echo "** Uploading Lita support files to remote host **"
scp ./uploads/* root@$DROPLET_HOST:~
scp ./slack_token_tmp.txt root@$DROPLET_HOST:/opt/lita_slack_token.txt
rm ./slack_token_tmp.txt

ssh root@$DROPLET_HOST "./install_dependencies.sh"
```

The server bootstrapping script makes heavy use of the echo command as a form of interactive documentation. A few things you should know about this script:

- The script assumes it's running on your local machine with the goal of setting up your remote Ubuntu Docker host machine.

- It assumes you have SSH and scp (secure file copy over SSH) installed locally and on the target server. You will if you're running OSX or Linux locally, and you definitely should have it on your target VPS.

- It interactively reads in your remote host's hostname or IP address to make its connection.

- It asks you for a Slack token for publishing your bot to a Slack channel. If you're looking to publish your bot to IRC or somewhere else, you'll have to adjust your scripts accordingly.

- It copies the rest of your server setup scripts to the remote Linux server and then kicks off the "install dependencies" script, which should take you all the way to the finish.

Before running this bootstrap script, you need to copy the three other scripts. The next few sections detail the contents of those three scripts. Once you have those, you'll be ready to kick things off.

Install operating system dependencies

This dependency installer script has a few distinct goals:

- Install the operating system dependencies required to meet your short-term goals. The Redis server is a Lita requirement, and the make command provides a simple dependency-based syntax for building and operating your Lita Docker containers from the command line.

- The make run command uses the Makefile you'll type up in the next section to download and start your Lita container. You'll pull your container image from a prebuilt copy on Docker Hub.

- A crontab command loads your final file—lita_crontab—into the system's scheduler. This runs once an hour to rebuild your docker container from Docker Hub and provides a way for you to keep your deployed bot up to date with a one-liner. You may want to set up a more sophisticated push-based updater that applies container updates quicker.

- The make log command demonstrates basic Docker logging, and it gives you a confirmation that your install process has successfully completed.

deploy-via-docker/uploads/install_dependencies.sh
```sh
#!/usr/bin/env sh

echo "** Installing OS Dependencies **"

# lita needs redis
apt-get install redis-server -qy

# your daemon script needs this
apt-get install make -qy

echo "** Installing Lita and starting it! **"
make run

echo "** Scheduling Lita to Rebuild from Docker Hub Hourly **"
crontab ./lita_crontab

echo "** Done! Waiting 5 seconds then showing docker logs. **"

sleep 5
make log
```

Your dependency installer gets copied from your local machine to the remote Linux server and then is executed using your top-level bootstrap script. The next section explains the Makefile.

Manage Lita container setup with the Makefile

The Makefile packages up the bot management lifecycle into a few tasks. Each is a one-liner with parameters that aren't necessarily easy to remember, so it's best to wrap them up as one-word make tasks:

- pull grabs the latest version of your Lita bot's Docker image from the public Docker hub.

- stop kills the running Lita process.

- destroy removes the existing latest container image for your Dockerized chatbot, clearing a space for you to pull the latest image in its place.

- run starts your bot as a background daemon using Docker.

- rebuild is a catch-all command that downloads the latest version of your bot (pull), removes the existing version (destroy), and starts the new one.

- log is an easy way to view the live output of your bot for debugging and health check purposes.

You can run make log or make rebuild from the Linux prompt whenever you want. The dependency installer script from the previous section explicitly requires only the run and log tasks. At the top of your Makefile, you'll see spot for you to enter environment-specific variables, like the path to your Docker hub image—or my reference image[4] if you decide not to create your own Dockerfile.

Why use a Makefile for a chatbot?

The make tool uses a Makefile to define a series of related commands to achieve a goal. While the goal is usually to compile a binary output file, such as a C++ executable, Make is quite serviceable as a general purpose workflow tool.

This is a nice fit for the small-to-medium build and deploy tasks that grow up around any command-line based tooling. Because the commonly repeated operations of managing a Docker-packaged chatbot are a series of interrelated one-liners like "download," "run," and "rebuild," make is an appropriate task runner.

---

4. https://github.com/dpritchett/ruby-bookbot/blob/master/Dockerfile

```
deploy-via-docker/uploads/Makefile
SLACK_TOKEN := $(shell cat /opt/lita_slack_token.txt)
IMAGE_NAME := lita_latest
DOCKER_HUB_IMAGE := dpritchett/ruby-bookbot:latest

rebuild: pull destroy run

pull:
        docker pull ${DOCKER_HUB_IMAGE}

stop:
        docker stop ${IMAGE_NAME}

destroy: stop
        docker rm ${IMAGE_NAME}

log:
        docker logs -f ${IMAGE_NAME}

run: pull
        docker run -dit --net="host" \
          -e "REDIS_URL=redis://localhost:6379" \
          -e "RACK_ENV=production" \
          -e "SLACK_TOKEN=${SLACK_TOKEN}" \
          --name ${IMAGE_NAME} ${DOCKER_HUB_IMAGE} \
            /bin/bash -c "cd /app && bundle exec lita" \
          --restart always --rm
```

Once you have your Makefile, there's one file left to set up: the crontab entry.

Schedule updates and restarts with your Crontab

Crontab is a Unix utility that provides individual users a place to register their own schedules for executing background jobs. In this case, you'll use a crontab file to schedule an hourly rebuild of your Lita bot's docker image.

```
deploy-via-docker/uploads/lita_crontab
# refresh and restart lita hourly
@hourly cd /root && make rebuild 2>&1 | logger -t LitaDaemon
```

This concise schedule entry might be difficult to read if you're not an experienced Linux administrator. Here are the parts and their meanings:

- @hourly: The task described on this line is intended to be run every hour on the hour.

- cd /root: Move to the root user's home directory before starting the job.

- &&: Chain a command after the previous one (i.e., stay in the root folder from the previous command to kick off the next one).

- make rebuild: Call the rebuild command from your Makefile, which is configured to stop, kill, and reload your Lita container.

- 2>&1: Send both STDOUT and STDERR logs to the main output.

- |: Pipe the output of the previous command (make rebuild) to the next command after the pipe operator (the vertical bar).

- logger -t LitaDaemon: Take incoming text out of the pipe and send it to logger, tagging each log line as belonging to LitaDaemon.

To tie all that together: You're scheduling an hourly task. It rebuilds your bot, gathers up its regular output and its error output into a single stream, and sends that log stream over to the logger command so that you'll be able to see it at any time in /var/log/syslog. This is a common pattern for Linux background services that you aren't likely to observe 24/7 but will undoubtedly want to debug from time to time.

Review Your Dockerized Bot through SSH

Now that your bot is downloaded, started, and scheduled to self update hourly by cron, you can log in to your Linux server and poke around to confirm everything's in order:

```
daniel@localhost: > ssh root@198.199.79.133
Welcome to Ubuntu 18.04.1 LTS (GNU/Linux 4.15.0-36-generic x86_64)

root@docker-s-1vcpu-1gb-nyc1-01:~# make log
docker logs -f lita_latest
[2018-10-05 15:15:53 UTC] INFO: Connected to Slack.

root@docker-s-1vcpu-1gb-nyc1-01:~# grep LitaDaemon /var/log/syslog
# nothing shows up yet because the hourly rebuild job hasn't happened
```

These snippets demonstrate logging into the Linux server, checking the Docker logs for your Lita bot, and then checking the syslog to see where potential issues will show up if your timed rebuild goes astray.

Wrap-up

In this chapter, you learned how to package your Lita bot as a Docker container, how to set up that dockerized Lita bot as an always-on service on a Linux host, and how to manage the daemon in case of future upgrades or service needs.

In the next chapter, you'll look at a more complex Lita interaction—web scraping—and you'll also get a chance to practice the general programming skill of planning out distinct conceptual and functional units within your code that work together smoothly.

Challenges

- This chapter has you using the Dockerfile that came with this book. It's common practice for operators of Docker-based services to manage their own Dockerfiles. Take a look at the official Dockerfile reference.[5] This should give you a feel for the commands used in the pre-configured Dockerfile referenced in this chapter.

- Confident sysadmins may prefer to deploy Lita without using Docker. If that's you, try using a tool like upstart to manage your Lita process as a natively running Ruby application on your own server.

- Lita's needs for a Redis server are pretty modest. Look into a simple hosted Redis solution like Redis Cloud. Try setting up your own remote Redis server and then tweaking your lita_config.rb[6] to connect to that remote server instead of a self-managed Redis.

- DigitalOcean is far from the only Docker-capable hosting platform. If you have a different preferred platform, try to reproduce this Lita setup on another Docker-oriented platform like Amazon's Elastic Container Service.

---

5. https://docs.docker.com/engine/reference/builder/
6. https://docs.lita.io/getting-started/configuration/

## CHAPTER 5

Parse a Photoblog: What's Brad Eating?

It's common for bot users to ask questions with image-oriented results. It's even more common for them to ask questions that are best answered by scraping a web page and pulling out a specific piece of the target site's content.

In this chapter, you'll pull in the top photo and caption from a food blog named, *What's Brad Eating? What's Brad Eating?* is a long-running tumblr from Pythonista and endurance athlete, Brad Montgomery; its theme: Regular photos of Brad's latest meal with captions describing the food.

The following image is a snapshot of the front page of *What's Brad Eating?*

To begin, you'll design an abstract question-and-answer-style interaction and figure out the different pieces that need to be implemented. You'll validate each piece by hand, and then safeguard things with some unit tests. Armed with the necessary building blocks, you'll construct the complete bot skill and test it out.

In working through this chapter, you'll learn two things: how to pull meaningful data out of any web page for the benefit of your bot's users, and how to approach skill development by breaking things down into individually manageable bits of Ruby.

Veteran programmers are likely familiar with the beginner's tendency to try to solve an entire problem in a single pass with a single brittle solution. This chapter walks through the analysis and building process piece by piece, so there's no temptation to skip to the end.

Build a Web Page Scraper Skill

Start with the expected interaction: Ask Lita, "what's brad eating" and get back the latest image URL and caption from Brad's tumblr.

```
Lita > lita what's brad eating
#eggs #avocado #breakfast >>
 https://68.media.tumblr.com/ccdb/tumblr_onoj_1280.jpg
```

In some contexts, you might feel motivated to render that image URL by wrapping it in some carefully crafted HTML. However, that's not necessary on most modern chat clients. Sending a JPEG link in a chat message achieves the desired effect as the client automatically renders the file in line.

A handful of distinct steps is required to achieve the desired effect, and you'll work through them one at a time. While "go find the latest from this blog" is the sort of business requirement a new project might start with, the step-by-step process it implies is a bit wordier.

Given the URL for a blog's front page, the tasks ahead look like this:

- Download that URL as an HTML payload.
- Parse that HTML into a structured format you can tease apart in Ruby.
- Isolate the latest post using a CSS selector query.
- Extract the image URL from the post.
- Extract the caption from the post.
- Format and return the results to the end user.

Building a new Lita skill starts with running Lita's handler generator. Because this type of work is so finicky, answer "yes" to all of the testing and validation questions. Lita's going to generate a test file, which you'll be happy to have. Each successive component from the task list needs to be properly implemented and verified before the next component on the list can be done.

Generate this new handler in a sibling folder adjacent to your bot so that you can link directly to the local copy while building it. Once it's ready, you can push it to RubyGems and link to the public copy.

Next is the shell session you need to reproduce to get Lita to generate the empty shell of your new bot skill, complete with test files.

```
lita-whats-brad-eating/examples/000_create_gem.session
$ lita handler whats-brad-eating
Do you want to test your plugin on Travis CI?
  ("yes" or "no", default is "no") yes
Do you want to generate code coverage information with SimpleCov
  and Coveralls.io?
  ("yes" or "no", default is "no") yes
If your plugin's Git repository will be hosted on GitHub, build status
  and code coverage badges can be automatically added to your README.
Would you like to add these badges? ("yes" or "no", default is "no") yes
What is your GitHub username? dpritchett
      create  lita-whats-brad-eating/lib/lita/handlers/whats_brad_eating.rb
      create  lita-whats-brad-eating/lib/lita-whats-brad-eating.rb
      create  lita-whats-brad-eating/spec/lita/handlers/wha..._spec.rb
      create  lita-whats-brad-eating/spec/spec_helper.rb
      create  lita-whats-brad-eating/locales/en.yml
      create  lita-whats-brad-eating/templates/.gitkeep
      create  lita-whats-brad-eating/Gemfile
      create  lita-whats-brad-eating/lita-whats-brad-eating.gemspec
      create  lita-whats-brad-eating/.gitignore
      create  lita-whats-brad-eating/.travis.yml
      create  lita-whats-brad-eating/Rakefile
      create  lita-whats-brad-eating/README.md
If you plan to release this plugin as open source software,
  consider adding a LICENSE file to the root of the repository.
Common open source software licenses can be found at
  http://choosealicense.com/.
Remember, for badges to be displayed in your plugin's README,
  you must host your project on GitHub.
Additionally, you will need to configure the project on
  Travis CI and Coveralls.io.
```

Set Up a Matcher

For this skill's matching expression, use "what's brad eating." This expression works well for end users because it's simple and memorable. As a reminder, expect to see "route," "listener," and "matcher" used interchangeably to represent "which words Lita is listening for in this context."

> ## Parsing with CSS selectors can be brittle
>
> If you've done any web scraping, you've probably had some bad days where the site's layout shifted and you had to rebuild the parser from the ground up. This "small, testable pieces" style of program construction helps to isolate the inevitable risk into separate "get the content" and "understand the content" methods, so the impact of a future breakage is limited.

lita-whats-brad-eating/examples/001_routing.rb
```ruby
# from lita-whats-brad-eating/lib/lita/handlers/whats_brad_eating.rb
route /^what's brad eating$/i,
  :brad_eats,             # name of handler method
  command: true,          # lita handles this as a direct command
  help: {                 # help text for this method when you ask "lita help"
    "what's brad eating" => "latest post from brad's food tumblr"
  }

def brad_eats(response)
  response.reply 'Actual results coming soon!'
end
```

The routing regular expression is not case sensitive. It only insists on matching something that looks like, "Lita what's brad eating"—no extras.

To add the new skill to the local Lita bot, you first need to link the local copy of the new lita-whats-brad-eating gem into your bot's Gemfile. Add the following line:

lita-whats-brad-eating/examples/002_gemfile_include.rb
```ruby
# Gemfile

# keep handlers in sibling folders to start with
gem 'lita-whats-brad-eating', path: '../lita-whats-brad-eating'
```

This path directive is a bit uncommon: normally Ruby gems are assumed to come directly from Rubygems.org. For gem development purposes, it's often easier to point to a local path adjacent to your application. Rerun bundler to link the bot to the local skill's path.

```
Lita > lita what's brad eating
Actual content coming soon...
Lita >
```

Success. The skill's matcher works and the skeleton is in place. Now it's time to wire up a blog parser to find some food photos. But first, firm up the matcher with a few tests.

```
lita-whats-brad-eating/examples/003_route_spec.rb
# from lita-whats-brad-eating/spec/lita/handlers/whats_brad_eating_spec.rb

describe 'routes' do
  # respond to this input:
  it { is_expected.to route("Lita what's brad eating") }
  # ... and also this one!
  it { is_expected.to route("Lita what's BRAD eating") }
end
```

These are spec-style tests[1] that verify the bot is going to detect all of the
expected variations on "what's brad eating." When run, the test suite spins
up a copy of the bot skill and passes it some text. Your test's success or failure
hinges on whether or not the bot correctly routes input like "what's BrAD
eating" to this skill.

Download the Raw HTML with Tumblr

For this skill, you're going to use one of Lita's built-in HTTP functions to
download the raw HTML from Tumblr. http.get leverages the faraday gem to pull
a response from a remote server and return it as text.

Do a quick Faraday request to verify what you're working with: Start a pry[2]
session to load Faraday for some interactive exploration. Remember, this
won't work until after you've added pry to your Gemfile.

```
pry(main)> require 'faraday'
true
pry(main)> response = Faraday.get('https://whatsbradeating.tumblr.com')
  ... response snipped for brevity
pry(main)> response.body.class
String < Object
pry(main)> response.body.lines.first
"<!DOCTYPE html><script>var __pbpa = true;</script>
  <script>var translated_warning_string =
  'Warning: Never enter your Tumblr password unless \\u201c
  https://www.tumblr.com/login\\u201d\\x0ai"
  ... response snipped for brevity
```

Here, you've leveraged pry to explore and experience the Ruby libraries you'll
need for your skill. You can see how a successful Faraday get returns the
page's entire HTML as a string. This is a perfect first step.

---

1. http://rspec.info/
2. https://pryrepl.org/

> \// **Joe asks:**
> ⌣ # **What's Pry?**
>
> Pry is a gem that provides Ruby programmers a souped-up local interpreter. It's conceptually similar to the IRB that comes with every Ruby install, but it can give the user a bit more information and control out of the box. The Ruby on Rails console has a lot in common with Pry—helpful colors, readable output, and convenience commands to make your job easier.

Time to bake in the "go get me that HTML" intention as a method in your handler. Below the matcher definition, shown earlier, add the following lita-whats-brad-eating/lib/lita/handlers/whats_brad_eating.rb. The skill uses the :response method to grab a copy of the blog's HTML once. It then saves it in memory. This saved HTML is available for reading throughout the Lita input handling cycle.

```ruby
# lita-whats-brad-eating/lib/lita/handlers/whats_brad_eating.rb
# hardcode the content source URL for reuse through the module
BLOG_URL = 'https://whatsbradeating.tumblr.com'.freeze

# save brad's web response for reuse in building your chat response
def response
  @_response ||= http.get(BLOG_URL)
end
```

This snippet pulls down the blog HTML and stores it in a string. Don't be tripped up by the @_ and ||= operators—they're common Ruby idioms. The first one, @_, is shorthand for "this is a useful instance variable but the underscore says I don't expect you to call it directly often." You can see the same thing in lots of Python code with leading single or double underscores for internally oriented variables and methods. The ||= (pronounced "or equals") operator assigns a new value to @_response only if no "truthy" valuable is already stored there. In short, you're going to pull down the blog's HTML from tumblr—once and only once—per instantiation of the WhatsBradEating handler class. You don't want repetitive calls to :response to re-download the page unnecessarily, particularly when you start writing fairly redundant tests.

Verify your progress with a test:

```ruby
# lita-whats-brad-eating/spec/lita/handlers/whats_brad_eating_spec.rb
# validate your basic HTML content fetching methods
describe ':response' do
  let(:body) { subject.response.body }

  it "should be able to pull down some HTML from Brad's blog" do
    expect(body =~ /<html>/i).to be_truthy
  end
end
```

```
  it 'should include something that looks like an image tag' do
    expect(body =~ /img src/i).to be_truthy
  end

  it 'should include a caption' do
    expect(body.include?('caption')).to be_truthy
  end
end
```

Execute these tests with rspec spec to see whether each of them pass. If you get zero errors, you're on the right track. If not, review the failure and see whether you've made a typo or skipped a step. As a last resort, you can look up the full implementation in the whats-brad-eating folder under the code listings distributed with this book.

Parse the Raw HTML with Nokogiri

Nokogiri is a popular Ruby gem that wraps the Libxml2 library and is what you'll use to parse the raw HTML data. Libxml2 is written in C to provide an efficient set of tools for XML parsing. It can be leveraged by slower, kinder languages like Ruby. If someone wants to programmatically access something that looks like markup, and they're in Ruby land, they're probably using Nokogiri.

For this, you're going to treat it a bit like JQuery: Given that you parsed some HTML, and you know the CSS selectors for the content you want to expose, you'll ask Nokogiri to fetch it for you using its :css method.

It's time for another pry session to prototype out the Nokogiri calls you need: "I have a big HTML string. I need you to parse it into a structured format so I can search for specific pieces and extract them for further use."

lita-whats-brad-eating/examples/004_faraday_log.rb
```
# load two gems to enable fetching and parsing of web content
pry(main)> require 'faraday'
true
pry(main)> require 'nokogiri'
true
pry(main)> raw_response = Faraday
  .get('https://whatsbradeating.tumblr.com').body;

pry(main)> parsed_response = Nokogiri.parse(raw_response)
# ... response snipped for brevity

pry(main)> parsed_response.class
Nokogiri::HTML::Document < Nokogiri::XML::Document
pry(main)> parsed_response.css('.post').first
# <Nokogiri::XML::Element:0x3fe00cd4a48c name="section"
#   attributes=[#<Nokogiri::XML::Attr:0x3fe00 name="class" value="post">]
#   children=[#<Nokogiri::XML::Text:0x3fe00a301a90 "\r\n
```

```
#    \r\n\r\n                                                \r\n
#    ">, #<Nokogiri::XML::Element:0x3fe00a3019dc name="
# ... remaining response snipped for brevity
```

This proves Nokogiri can parse the HTML string representing the front page of Brad's tumblr and that you get a Nokogiri::XML::Document as a return value.

Here's the simple parsing with Nokogiri.parse. Add it to the whats-brad-eating.rb file, along with your matcher and the other components.

```
def parsed_response
  Nokogiri.parse(response.body) # returns a nokogiri Document object
end
```

Here's the validation that you have a parsed object that allows you to find HTML elements with CSS selectors. Add it to whats-brad-eating-spec.rb.

```
lita-whats-brad-eating/spec/lita/handlers/whats_brad_eating_spec.rb
# validate navigability of parsed web content
describe ':parsed_response' do
  it 'should return a nokogiri object with a :css method we can search on' do
    expect(subject.parsed_response).to respond_to(:css)

    images = subject.parsed_response.css('img')
    expect(images.any?).to be_truthy
  end
end
```

Isolate the First Post with a CSS Selector

Chrome Dev Tools is an efficient way to isolate the CSS selectors required to target the post with Nokogiri. The following image shows the post element in place as a DOM element.

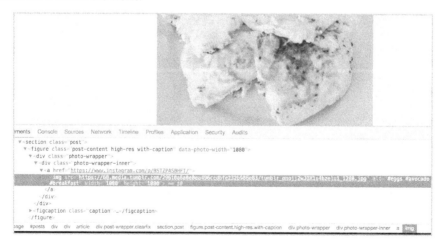

The status bar shows a top-down navigation path from the body down through an element with a .post CSS class. The .post contains a <section>, which in turn, contains a .photo-wrapper. At the tip of this branch of the document lives the <img> tag that Lita needs.

The image URL and the caption are both available as attributes of the targeted image. If you're looking to reproduce this at home—on a different site—right-click the targeted element. Then, click *Inspect* (in Chrome) to open the inspector view with a focus on the selected page element. Eyeballing the CSS selectors Chrome has unearthed for you, try to isolate the first post with a call to Nokogiri's :css method scoped to look inside of the section.post DOM object.

Here's the implementation for a method to isolate the first post:

```
def first_post
  parsed_response.css('section.post').first
end
```

And here's the test to prove it out:

```
describe ':first_post' do
  it 'finds exactly one node' do
    expect(subject.first_post.count).to eq(1)
  end
end
```

Now that you've isolated the first post, you can dig out the image with its photo URL and caption metadata.

Find the Image with Another CSS Selector

Nokogiri lets you chain :css calls. Starting with first_post, which returned a Nokogiri::XML::Node, you're going to dig in for its first img element. Check in on that pry session to see what you have to work with.

```
# pp 'pretty prints' a data structure to be more human readable
pry(main)> pp parsed_response.css('section.post').first.css('img').first

#(Element:0x3fe00a300334 {
  name = "img",
  attributes = [
    #(Attr:0x3fe00a3002d0 {
      name = "src",
      value = "https://68.media.tumblr.com/ccd/tumblr_ono_1280.jpg"
      }),
    #(Attr:0x3fe00a3002bc {
      name = "alt",
      value = "#eggs #avocado #breakfast"
      }),
... snipped remainder of response for brevity
```

The image caption is embedded in its alt attribute and its photo URL in its src attribute. Once you dig out attributes from a Nokogiri object, you're home free.

Here's the "isolate the image element" implementation:

```
def image
  first_post.css(".photo-wrapper img").first
end
```

And here's the test for the isolated image:

```
lita-whats-brad-eating/spec/lita/handlers/whats_brad_eating_spec.rb
describe ':image' do
  it 'finds at least one node' do
    attributes = subject.image.attributes
    expect(attributes.fetch('src').value).to include('http')

    # captions could be anything, let's just verify we got one
    expect(attributes.key?('alt')).to be_truthy
  end
end
```

Format the Results to Share with the End User

Now that you have the image, URL, and caption, all that's left to do is slap it all together in the top-level :brad_eats handler method and call it a day.

```
lita-whats-brad-eating/lib/lita/handlers/whats_brad_eating.rb
# load up the caption and image using the methods above
#    and send them back to the chat room
def brad_eats(response)
  # caption text had some stray newlines we don't need
  caption_text = caption.text.strip
  img_url = image.get_attribute('src')

  msg = "#{caption_text} >> #{img_url}"

  response.reply msg
end
```

You need one final end-to-end test to verify that the entire pipeline works. The next snippet sends a "what's brad eating" command to Lita and checks the text output for the expected image caption and URL.

```
lita-whats-brad-eating/spec/lita/handlers/whats_brad_eating_spec.rb
# high-level "lita hears X and returns Y" end-to-end testing
describe ':brad_eats' do
  it 'responds with a caption and an image URL' do
    send_message "Lita what's brad eating"
    expect(replies.last).to match(/\w+ >> http/i)
  end
end
```

Run rspec spec one last time (10 examples, 0 failures) and try out the results.

```
Lita > lita what's brad eating
#eggs #avocado #breakfast >>
 https://68.media.tumblr.com/ccdb/tumblr_onojj_1280.jpg
```

The following image depicts a Lita bot successfully displaying Brad's breakfast in Slack.

Perhaps it's time for you to celebrate with a nice meal. Do you like eggs?

Wrap-up

By completing this chapter, you learned how to pull in meaningful content from structured web pages. Not just Tumblr—any page with a consistent layout from one item to the next is now yours for the scraping.

You also explored the benefits of breaking down chatbot programming problems into bite-sized chunks and testing the chunks. After you get that down, it's comparatively easy to assemble a finished product out of your tested code chunks.

Up next is a variation on the parsing skills you used in this chapter. Rather than parse raw, browser-oriented HTML directly, you'll pull in data from the Meetup.com event planning API. You'll get a Meetup API key and learn how to query Meetup's API for upcoming events in your area. Once you've automated the process of pulling and parsing Meetup's event planning API results, you'll serve them up to your bot's users as another chat-based service.

Challenges

Here are some challenges you can try on your own:

- *Parse a different blog*: Pick another photoblog with consistent styling and content. Can you use the techniques in this chapter to parse the blog with your bot?

- *Mess with the images before you render them*: Once you have an image URL, send it back out to a silly image overlay service like a mustachifier or an "add silly meme text here" service.

- *Two-site mashup*: Can you juxtapose the content of one blog with another? Try pulling the top three headlines from your most favorite political news site, and then again from your least favorite. Compare the two and spend the next few minutes shaking your fist at the sky.

## CHAPTER 6

Meetup Finder

Meetups are a popular way to meet and bond with like-minded individuals nearby, and chatbot skills are a common and effective way to share this type of calendar information with community members.

The following image shows the Meetup.com search results for "dancing" meetups near Memphis.

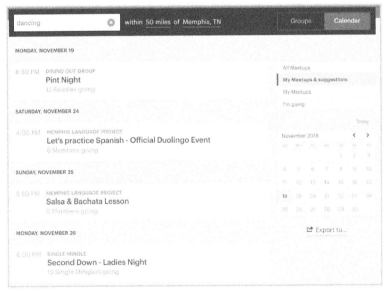

In this chapter, you'll learn how to write a skill that queries the Meetup.com calendar API for upcoming local interest group meetups near you. For example:

> **Lita find meetup climbing**

```
Grivet Outdoors:  Hiking Trip to Pinnacle Mountain  >> Group: Memphis
  Outdoor Adventures >> Sun Nov 11 07:00:00 2018
    >> https://www.meetup.com/MemphisOutdoors/events/255648545/
```

Set Up a Meetup.com Account and API Key

Before you can work with the Meetup API, you need to register for an account. From the Sign up link in the Meetup.com header, you can register using a personal email, a Google account, or a Facebook account. Once logged in, locate meetup.com's Getting an API Key[1] page to create your own key. The generated key will look something like this: 14ae7022223d49b6e5e673d3e29.

Although Meetup has a full-featured API that enables many different integrations, you only need one API action for this chapter: GET open_events. For more information about the Meetup API, review the Meetup documentation.[2]

You're ready to create your next Lita handler.

Connect to the Meetup API Using the Meetup Client Gem

To generate a Lita handler at the console, use lita handler meetup-finder. This creates a new lita-meetup-finder directory, complete with a gemspec, a README file, and the rest of the skeleton for a new Lita skill.

Open your new lita-meetup-finder directory and type the following meetup_client in the runtime dependencies section. This gives you access to the Meetup API through Ruby.

lita-meetup-finder/lita-meetup-finder.gemspec
```
spec.add_runtime_dependency 'meetup_client', '~> 1.0'
```

You also need a development dependency named webmock. Webmock is a huge productivity booster when developing against external APIs. With it, you can hack your test suite. In other words, tests that call out to external services—in this case, the meetup.com API—are intercepted and handled with a set of prerecorded responses rather than making the external call. This is helpful for two reasons: First, it limits the number of times you hit meetup.com's API with identical requests while you're developing—this is great because API providers typically don't appreciate clients who ask the same question repeatedly. Second, and perhaps more helpful, webmock's prerecorded responses to HTTP calls allow for more deterministic testing. For example, every time your test code asks the meetup API, "what climbing-related meetups are available this week?" it gets the same response. You can now write more precise tests because the API responses are quick and consistent. If the Meetup API changes, you can capture a new response to your test question

---

1.   https://secure.meetup.com/meetup_api/key/

2.   https://www.meetup.com/meetup_api/

and save that for WebMock to use for future tests. Add WebMock to the development dependencies section of lita-meetup-finder.gemspec:

lita-meetup-finder/lita-meetup-finder.gemspec
```
spec.add_development_dependency 'webmock', '~> 3.3'
```

With both meetup_client and webmock added, you're ready to run bundle to install all of the dependencies required for this skill.

Teach Lita How to Query the Meetup API

Your meetup finder skill has two major components: a standard Lita handler layer to connect chat users with the meetup API and a model class for standardizing parsing of the meetup API responses. You'll start with the Lita handler layer.

Open your meetup_finder.rb implementation and add the required meetup_client gem at the top of the file:

lita-meetup-finder/lib/lita/handlers/meetup_finder.rb
```
# Load 3rd party meetup API client gem
require 'meetup_client'
```

Next, you'll set up a handy convention for wrapping normal exceptions in the course of interacting with a remote API.

Create a custom API error class

API clients tend to fail in predictable ways, such as:

- Bad or missing API key
- Unable to connect to the remote API (maybe your Wi-Fi is down?)
- No results found (probably not an exception, just business logic)
- Unrecognized response format from remote API

By giving yourself a common ApiError class, you're able to quickly tell (by eyeballing a stack trace or a midnight alert email) that an error is localized to an API client. So, with that in mind, you'll catch expected failure cases and wrap them in your custom error class.

Open the MeetupFinder class and set up a custom error handling class named MeetupApiError. Here's a demo of a custom error class in action:

```
lita-meetup-finder/examples/002-simple-error.session
dpritchett@Neuromancer ~> pry
[1] pry(main)> ClassUnfinishedError = Class.new(StandardError)
=> ClassUnfinishedError
[2] pry(main)> class DemonstratesErrors
[2] pry(main)*   def initialize
                    message = "Whoops, this class is unfinished!"
[2] pry(main)*     raise ClassUnfinishedError.new message
[2] pry(main)*   end
[2] pry(main)* end
=> :initialize
[3] pry(main)> DemonstratesErrors.new
ClassUnfinishedError: Whoops, this class is unfinished!
from (pry):4:in `initialize'
[4] pry(main)>
```

Add Meetup-specific keys to the Lita configuration object

Lita handlers—like your Meetup finder—are distributed to end users as
RubyGems, so your code needs a way to receive per-install configuration
options, like Meetup API keys and local zip codes through a common format.
With Lita bots, that's done using the Lita#config method:

```
lita-meetup-finder/lib/lita/handlers/meetup_finder.rb
# Set these in your bot's lita_config.rb or via environment
#   variable
config :meetup_api_key, default: ENV['MEETUP_API_KEY']
# note the
config :meetup_zip, default: ENV['MEETUP_ZIP']
```

Next, you'll declare two configuration options named MEETUP_API_KEY and MEET-
UP_ZIP. With these options in place, end users can configure via their own
lita_config.rb files for their local bot installs. As usual, you'll have a fallback that
hits an operating system environment variable to allow runtime injection of
these values:

```
lita-meetup-finder/examples/001-runtime-env-var.sh
$ env MEETUP_API_KEY='14ae7022223d49b6e5e673d3e29' MEETUP_ZIP='38117' lita
Type "exit" or "quit" to end the session.
Lita > lita find meetup python
Memphis Python User Group >> Group: Memphis Technology User Groups
 >> Mon Nov 19 18:30:00 2018
 >> https://www.meetup.com/memphis-technology-user-groups/events/255343667/
```

The previous example shows the "specify my config via environment variables
at runtime" option. This may be preferable in certain deployment scenarios,
for instance, a Kubernetes-hosted bot.

Capture a "lita find meetup ___" route

This chapter's text route handler is fairly standard: It looks for text matching "Lita find Meetup search_term_goes_here":

Is regex the right way to parse natural languages?

lita-meetup-finder/lib/lita/handlers/meetup_finder.rb
```
route(/^find meetup\s+(.+)$/i, :find_matching_meetup, command: true)
```

The route method registers your regular expression with Lita, the regex itself confirms that you want to match strings that begin with "find meetup," have some whitespace, and end with a search term. This code opts for a case-insensitive route by ending the regex with /i. The command: true directive informs Lita not to respond to overheard notes like find meetup x but only to queries directly addressed to your bot.

Handle user input and provide basic responses

Next is the method that finds matching meetups. This is your core handler method that the route from the previous section invokes. Like any Lita handler method, you'll start from a message object that contains a :matches object of the user inputs that triggered your handler. You'll grab the first match out of your match data structure and pass it along to your as-yet-unwritten meetups_matching method:

lita-meetup-finder/lib/lita/handlers/meetup_finder.rb
```
def find_matching_meetup(message)
  # extract search term from user input
  search_term = message.matches.first
  # pass search term to meetup query method
  meetups = meetups_matching search_term

  # handle two basic outcomes: no results, 1+ results
  if meetups.none?
    message.reply "Sorry, no matching meetups found."
  else
    message.reply meetups.first&.tagline
  end
end
```

Assuming you get back search results, you'll send them back to your chat user via message.reply. If there are no results, you can send back a boilerplate response, such as "no meetups found." Note that this method is plain Ruby logic; all of the API-specific bits are wrapped up in another method. This style of decomposing a class into small, single-purpose methods will serve you well when building future Lita skills or when programming in general.

Configure the Meetup client class with API credentials

Lita's interactions with the Meetup API need to pass through the required meetup_client gem. While your key interaction is nothing more than a call to the open_events method, you'll need to expose a Meetup API client to your Lita handler.

The following client method sets up a pre-configured API client with Lita's Meetup API key pre-filled. Note that the @_client ||= idiom is a way to cache a reusable connection for the duration of a Lita interaction, rather than having to recreate the client on every call to :client. The @_ represents a persistent instance variable that is not intended to be called directly, as opposed to, say, a @client variable:

```
lita-meetup-finder/lib/lita/handlers/meetup_finder.rb
def client
  MeetupClient.configure do |meetup_config|
    # sets meetup config using value from lita config
    meetup_config.api_key = config.meetup_api_key
  end

  # store client rather than rebuilding on each call
  @_client ||= MeetupApi.new
end
```

Scour the Meetup API for a specific search term

At this point in your handler file, you have access to a logged-in Meetup API client and a query string extracted from your end user's "lita find meetup clowns" query. The following :meetups_matching method builds on that foundation by constructing a Meetup-formatted search query payload and then inspecting the results to see whether there's something worth sending back to the chat room. The :build_search method (covered next) turns a query like "lita find meetup clowns" into the :open_events API payload format that's required to grab the info you need out of Meetup's API.

Note that the actual call to the external API and the immediate review of the API response are both wrapped in a begin/rescue StandardError block, which should catch the common failure cases of "Meetup doesn't like my API key," "Meetup can't be found on my network," and "Meetup sent back an unexpected response."

Here's part of a sample Meetup JSON response. Take a look at the structure of the payload. Later in the chapter, you'll write a custom model class to handle these responses.

lita-meetup-finder/examples/003-meetup-response.json
```json
{
    "results":[
        {
            "utc_offset":-21600000,
            "venue":{
                "zip":"38104",
                "country":"us",
                "localized_country_name":"USA",
                "city":"Memphis",
                "address_1":"2164 Young Ave",
                "name":"Grivet Outdoors",
                "lon":-89.990074,
                "id":25963887,
                "state":"tn",
                "lat":35.119804,
                "repinned":true
            },
            "headcount":0,
# rest of the payload is omitted for readability...
```

The final line of this search method passes all of the JSON results from the Meetup API to a separate class that you'll write soon: MeetupResult. This is the Plain Old Ruby Object (PORO) that gives you a convenient and maintainable Ruby interface to the Meetup-formatted JSON payload:

lita-meetup-finder/lib/lita/handlers/meetup_finder.rb
```ruby
# query Meetup API for local meetups and return a
#    list of matching MeetupResult objects
def meetups_matching(search_text)
  query = build_search(search_text)

  begin
    response = client.open_events(query)
    results = response.fetch('results')
  rescue StandardError
    raise MeetupApiError.new(response)
  end

  # coerce an array of JSON-ish results into richer
  #    MeetupResult objects
  results.map { |r| MeetupResult.new(r) }
end
```

Prepare a hashmap with Meetup-compliant search parameters

The :build_search method is straightforward. It takes in a search_text, grabs your Lita-config-provided meetup_zip, and packages them in a four-term hashmap that matches the format demanded by Meetup.com's open_events endpoint:

```
lita-meetup-finder/lib/lita/handlers/meetup_finder.rb
  def build_search(search_text)
    {
      zip: config.meetup_zip,
      format: 'json',
      page: '5',
      text: search_text
    }
end
```

This covers all of the logic that's required to capture a user's intent to find a specific meetup, pass it along to Meetup.com as a query, and then send the meetups returned by the API back to the chat users. In the next section, you'll work through the MeetupResponse model class and get some practice building a Plain Old Ruby Object (PORO) around a JSON payload. Later in this chapter, you'll learn more about POROs.

Test Your MeetupFinder Class

You're going to take a break from the back-and-forth cadence of test-driven development to make room for a bit of setup on WebMock. You learned earlier that WebMock helps you write simpler, more useful tests around your calls to the Meetup API. However, to make that happen, you need to add some WebMock-specific configuration to your RSpec setup.

The first step to make WebMock happen is to crack open your spec_helper file and require WebMock's RSpec module at the top of the file:

```
lita-meetup-finder/spec/spec_helper.rb
require 'webmock/rspec'
```

You're now ready to define a stub-out-external-API-calls method just for Meetup's API:

```
lita-meetup-finder/spec/spec_helper.rb
# call me in a before block anywhere you're calling pastebin!
#   This will save you from fairly low-overhead API limits.
def stub_meetup_calls!
    stub_request(:get, /api.meetup.com/).
    with(
      headers: {
        'Accept'=>'*/*',
        'Accept-Charset'=>'UTF-8',
        'Accept-Encoding'=>'gzip;q=1.0,deflate;q=0.6,identity;q=0.3',
        'User-Agent'=>'Ruby'
      }).
    to_return(status: 200, body: json_fixture, headers: {})
end
```

You'll use that "stub meetup" method in your specs as a way of short-circuiting any calls to api.meetup.com and substituting a pre-recorded response. You can capture your own JSON response to use as a fixture or you can skip that and dig out the fixture that comes with this book's code listings as spec/fixtures/meetup_results.json. Note the call to :json_fixture at the tail end of the stub method:

lita-meetup-finder/spec/spec_helper.rb
```
def json_fixture
  @_raw_json ||= open('./spec/fixtures/meetup_results.json')
end
```

This :json_fixture method loads up a plain-text JSON file and hands it off to WebMock to send back to your calling code (the MeetupFinder class) instead of an actual live API response. While this book's code listings provide a sample payload for you to use, you can always generate a new payload by firing up a MeetupApi client in a pry session and capturing the response you get back from a valid :open_events request.

Your file for the MeetupFinder class needs to invoke the stub_meetup_calls! method before every test:

lita-meetup-finder/spec/lita/handlers/meetup_finder_spec.rb
```
describe Lita::Handlers::MeetupFinder, lita_handler: true do
  subject { described_class.new(robot) }

  # Ask webmock to intercept any HTTP traffic to meetup API
  #  and respond with stored data instead of live data
  before { stub_meetup_calls! }
```

On top of short-circuiting all calls to Meetup.com, you need to pre-fill your test Lita bot's config object with useful API key and ZIP code defaults using a before(:each) block:

lita-meetup-finder/spec/lita/handlers/meetup_finder_spec.rb
```
let(:test_api_key) { nil } ##'14ae7022223d49b6e5e673d3e29' }   ???
let(:test_zip) { 38117 }

# force config values to things you can test against
before(:each) do
    # you'll need your own test API key here
    subject.config.meetup_api_key = test_api_key
    subject.config.meetup_zip = test_zip
end
```

Now, you need to test your Meetup finder skill's chat routes with the expected.to route call. As usual, you'll test whether an unrelated query gets picked up by this specific handler's routes:

```
lita-meetup-finder/spec/lita/handlers/meetup_finder_spec.rb
describe 'routes' do
  # confirm three variations on what's brad eating each trigger a response
  it { is_expected.to route("Lita find meetup climbing") }
  it { is_expected.to_not route("Lita what's for dinner?") }
end
```

Your next test stanza confirms that the hash-map generated with :build_search conforms to the expectations set forth in Meetup's docs for :open_events. The word "climbers" goes in and a four-parameter hash comes out:

```
lita-meetup-finder/spec/lita/handlers/meetup_finder_spec.rb
describe ':build_search' do
    let(:search_text) { 'climbers' }
    let(:result) { subject.build_search search_text }

    it "should return a hash of Meetup search parameters" do
        expected = {
            zip: test_zip,
            format: 'json',
            page: '5',
            text: search_text
        }

        expect(result).to eq expected
    end
end
```

Next, test the core :meetup_search method to validate that a search for "climbers" returns the two meetups embedded in the JSON through WebMock:

```
lita-meetup-finder/spec/lita/handlers/meetup_finder_spec.rb
# validate your basic HTML content fetching methods
describe ':meetup_search' do
  let(:climbers) { subject.meetups_matching 'climbers' }

  it "should find two results" do
    expect(climbers.count).to eq(2)
  end
end
```

The final test for this validates end-to-end functionality: User asks "find meetup climbing" and Lita returns a URL with some adjacent formatting chevrons.

```
lita-meetup-finder/spec/lita/handlers/meetup_finder_spec.rb
# high-level "lita hears X and returns Y" end-to-end testing
describe ':meetup_find' do
  it 'responds with a list of relevant meetups' do
    send_message "Lita find meetup climbing"
    expect(replies.last).to match(/\w+ >> http/i)
  end
end
```

Model the API Response with a Plain Old Ruby Object

The model approach is handy when dealing with big JSON responses from remote APIs, because it helps the developer call out the parts of the response payload that are relevant to the calling module's business logic. In this case, the Meetup responses might have dozens of bits of information about any given meetup, but your chat room users only need a few of them. The approach you'll use to model this response payload is known as a Plain Old Ruby Object or PORO, as mentioned earlier. In other popular languages, you'll see POJOs[3] (Java) and POCOs (C#).

Next is the initialize method of your MeetupResult class. Ruby invokes this method whenever someone calls MeetupResult.new(json_payload_goes_here). The logic of this method is a series of assignments to instance variables. @raw_result captures the original input—always useful for debugging—which is crucial for unpacking the specific bits that are necessary for Lita to format a meetup listing in a couple of lines of plain text suitable for a chat room:

```
lita-meetup-finder/lib/lita/meetup_result.rb
def initialize(raw_result)
    @raw_result = raw_result

    @name = raw_result.fetch('name')
    @url = raw_result.fetch('event_url')
    @group_name = raw_result.fetch('group').fetch('name')
end
```

Using the :fetch method to dig out values of hashmap-formatted payloads serves a useful purpose here—you'll get KeyErrors in your log if the key you're hunting for is missing in a payload at runtime. Failing fast with a meaningful error like this is just what you want when trying to debug unexpected behavior in your Ruby bot. For a more in-depth explanation of the virtues of Hash#fetch, look at RubyTapas.[4]

After the :initialize/:new method has filled in these first four instance variables, you'll expose them all as read-only getter methods on your MeetupResult class with a call to :attr_reader:

```
lita-meetup-finder/lib/lita/meetup_result.rb
# expose instance variables as attribute getters
attr_reader :raw_result, :name, :url, :group_name
```

---

3. https://en.wikipedia.org/wiki/Plain_old_Java_object
4. https://www.rubytapas.com/2018/06/20/bust-nils-with-hash-fetch/

The Meetup API lists its event start and finish times as integers representing the number of milliseconds since the start of 1970 (a.k.a. the Unix Epoch), so you'll need to unpack human-readable dates from that integer. In the following method's comment, you can see how an integer time like 1541941200000 translates to early on November 11th, 2018. The Time#ctime call formats this integer time as a decidedly more human-friendly "Sun Nov 11 07:00:00 2018":

lita-meetup-finder/lib/lita/meetup_result.rb
```ruby
# Human readable start time for the event
#   Raw time:    1541941200000
#   Human time: Sun Nov 11 07:00:00 2018
def start_time
    # API results are in milliseconds since the unix epoch
    epoch_msec = raw_result.fetch('time')
    epoch_sec = epoch_msec / 1000

    Time.at(epoch_sec).ctime    ← time zone ?
end
```

The following :tagline method encapsulates the end user's only real interest in this MeetupResult object: It massages your Rubyfied JSON payload into a single string listing of the critical information of the meetup in question:

lita-meetup-finder/lib/lita/meetup_result.rb
```ruby
def tagline
    "#{name} >> Group: #{group_name} >> #{start_time} >> #{url}"
end
```

Test your MeetupResult class

Your MeetupResult's tests are straightforward. Start by providing the JSON fixture to your tests as a :raw_results object:

lita-meetup-finder/spec/lita/meetup_result_spec.rb
```ruby
describe Lita::MeetupResult do
  let(:raw_results) { JSON.load(json_fixture).fetch('results') }

  it "has a fixture with 2 results" do
    expect(raw_results.count).to eq 2
  end
```

To build on the :raw_results test, parse each result as a MeetupResult and expose those as the :parsed_results collection:

lita-meetup-finder/spec/lita/meetup_result_spec.rb
```ruby
context "Result parsing" do
  let(:parsed_results) { raw_results.map { |el| described_class.new el } }

  it "can parse the fixture's JSON input as MeetupResult objects" do
    expect(parsed_results.map(&:class).uniq).to eq [described_class]
  end
```

With the results parsed, all that's left to test is the shape of your MeetupResponse object. Does it have all of the accessors your Lita handler needs? Do they look the way you need them to look to fulfill end-user requests? Use this test to find out:

lita-meetup-finder/spec/lita/meetup_result_spec.rb
```ruby
context "accessor methods" do
  let(:result) { parsed_results.first }

  it 'parses group name' do
    expect(result.group_name).to eq "Memphis Outdoor Adventures"
  end

  it 'parses event name' do
    expect(result.name).to include 'Pinnacle Mountain'
  end

  it 'parses start time' do
    expect(result.start_time).to include 'Sun Nov 11'
  end

  it 'parses url' do
    expect(result.url.start_with? 'https://www.meetup.com/').to be_truthy
  end
```

So far, you tested all of your getter methods. All that remains is to confirm that the :tagline method doesn't throw an exception, and that its contents include the text of each of your accessor methods:

lita-meetup-finder/spec/lita/meetup_result_spec.rb
```ruby
context 'human-friendly formatting' do
  let(:tagline) { result.tagline }
  fields = [:group_name, :name, :start_time, :url]

  fields.each do |field|
    it "tagline includes #{field}" do
      expected = result.send(field)
      expect(tagline.include? expected).to be_truthy
    end
  end
end
end
```

You finished building and testing your MeetupFinder and MeetupResult classes, and your Lita handler is complete.

Upload your new skill to RubyGems

You're ready to upload your finished skill to RubyGems. At this point, git commit your latest work, and then run a rake release as described in Chapter 2, Your First Lita Skill, on page 9 to deploy your gem to RubyGems.

Wrap-up

In this chapter, you learned how to use a third-party API client to bring in outside information. This gives your Lita bot capabilities that would otherwise be a lot to build out yourself. You'll find that taking a query from chat and sending it to an external API is a common theme throughout this book. After implementing a few of these examples, you'll be ready to identify and integrate other useful APIs for your chatbot and your other programs.

This chapter's detours into POROs and WebMock are useful building blocks for larger challenges in your future. In the next chapter, you'll learn how to use the Imgflip API to create jokey meme images for your chat rooms.

Challenges

- Community-oriented Lita bots tend to have a few very common use cases. Find your favorite local meetup and build a new Lita chat route to look it up on Meetup directly. For instance, "Lita find Meetup Frisbee" should already be able to find your next local Frisbee-related meetup. Try making a "lita frisbee" route that calls the same logic behind the scenes.

- Meetup's "find events" API endpoint has several extra search options that this chapter didn't explore. Read over the official documentation for those[5] and see whether something doesn't jump out at you that might be useful to your Lita bot's user base.

- This chapter took the easy path to returning the first matching result to your chat room. Try adding extra Lita routing and handler logic to allow users to request more than one result. Do you want to ask for five results at once? Do you want to ask for the second or third result specifically?

---

5. https://www.meetup.com/meetup_api/docs/find/upcoming_events/

## CHAPTER 7

Imgflip Meme Maker

One of the more fun and rewarding chatbot integrations you can create for your community is a skill that generates whimsical meme images with a one-line command. Imagine that the user types, "Lita, one does not simply build a chatbot," and they're immediately rewarded with a picture of Tolkien's Boromir explaining the folly of the mission.

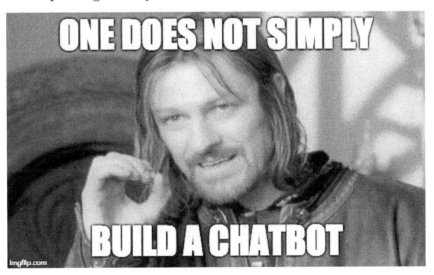

This *image macro* was created using the Imgflip API. An image macro is, to quote KnowYourMeme.com,[1] "a broad term used to describe captioned images that typically consist of a picture and a witty message or a catchphrase. On discussion forums and imageboards, image macros are also used to convey feelings or reactions toward another member of the community, similar to its predecessor emoticons."

---

1. http://knowyourmeme.com/memes/image-macros

In this chapter, you'll use Imgflip as the backend for the meme creator. (Note: I use meme and image macro interchangeably for this chapter.) Using the Imgflip API serves two educational purposes: it provides a simple enough means to create image-based jokes, and it provides your first look at integrating with an external API. The patterns established here will help you integrate your own external APIs if you should need to. You'll also have the opportunity to add some slightly more advanced regular expressions to your bot—good practice for future Lita work.

Make an Image Macro

The regular Imgflip experience is the web-based configuration tool. From the main imgflip,.com page you'll click *Create* and then *Caption a Meme*. On the resulting page, you select a background image macro template from the carousel on the right, type some text for the "top text" and "bottom text" inputs, click *Generate Meme*, and the site shows the finished image along with download and social sharing links.

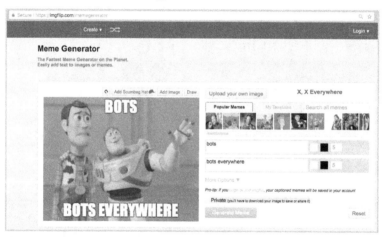

The Imgflip web interface is a great way to prototype new features before you code them into your Lita skill.

Using the Imgflip API

Imgflip's API uses the same HTTP techniques that web browsers use to communicate with web servers. That is, a client—like a browser or your bot—makes an HTTP POST request to Imgflip's servers. The POST asks the server to generate a new image macro. The new macro is expected to overlay the API client's specified text on the chosen image.

Look at the following sample Faraday JSON request. Remember, Faraday is the library that Lita uses under-the-hood to pull remote URLs.

```
Line 1  [1] pry(main)> require 'faraday'
        true
        [2] pry(main)> require 'json'
        true
     5  [3] pry(main)>
        [4] pry(main)> response = Faraday.post(
          'https://api.imgflip.com/caption_image',
        [4] pry(main)*   template_id: 101470,
        [4] pry(main)*   username: 'redacted',
    10  [4] pry(main)*   password: 'redacted',
        [4] pry(main)*   text0: '',
        [4] pry(main)*   text1: 'aliens')
        # most of the response object omitted for brevity
        #<Faraday::Response:0x007fad150238d8 @on_complete_callbacks=[],
    15   @env=#<Faraday::Env @method=:post
         @body='{\"success\":true,
           \"data\":{\"url\":\"http:\\/\\/i.imgflip.com\\/1u18ku.jpg\',
         @status=200, @reason_phrase="OK">>
        [5] pry(main)>
    20  [6] pry(main)> response.status
        200
        [7] pry(main)>
        [8] pry(main)> JSON.parse response.body
        {
    25     "success" => true,
             "data" => {
                   "url" => "http://i.imgflip.com/1u18ku.bbbbb",
               "page_url" => "https://imgflip.com/i/1u18ku"
           }
    30  }
```

For commands 1 and 2, you require faraday to make HTTP requests and json to parse the JSON-formatted response you expect from Imgflip (see the Imgflip API docs[2]). With the fourth command (Faraday.post), you call the Imgflip API directly at api.imgflip.com/caption_image.

Lines 7 through 12 show the POST request using the Faraday object. Note its inclusion of the five required parameters for an Imgflip macro. Lines 23 through 30 show the parsing of the Imgflip's JSON string response into a native Ruby hashmap object.

---

2. https://api.imgflip.com/

Prototype an API Request with Faraday

Imgflip requires at least five pieces of information to generate a captioned image:

- username**. To get one of these, sign up at https://imgflip.com/signup.

- password**. You'll need one when you sign up.

- *text0*. Image templates seem to all have two spots available in which to write text, mostly at the top and the bottom of the image. text0 is the top line. Even if you don't want a top line, you need to submit an empty string.

- *text1*. This is the bottom line. Empty strings work here as well.

- *Template id*. These are the prepared backgrounds that Imgflip prints captions over.

A list of the top 100 meme templates is at https://api.imgflip.com/popular_meme_ids. To find ids for less popular templates, you can browse the site directly or use the get_memes API described in Imgflip's docs. It doesn't seem quite as easy to dig up template IDs from the website directly, but it can be done by logging POST data when generating a meme.

Chrome Dev Tools view of an imgflip form submission. Note that the POST headers in the bottom-right panel include the template ID.

To request a specific meme, you need an Imgflip template id. The previous screenshot demonstrates that the POST headers sent by the browser on submit include a form field of template: 25926475. To track your own POSTs, you can open the developer toolbar in Chrome (View -> Developer -> Developer Tools) and then click the Network tab to track the POST when you submit a meme.

Process the API response

Line 6 of the Faraday example you saw earlier checks the HTTP response status code.[3] "200 OK" is good news—Imgflip accepted the request and returned a freshly generated image macro.

In line 8, Ruby converts the body of the HTTP response from JSON-encoded text to a native Ruby hashmap and stores it in the parsed variable. In the parsed payload is a data object containing a url key with a jpeg URL as its value—that's the generated image.

To summarize: you make a properly formed request to Imgflip's API using a template ID and some API credentials, and you get back the URL of an image macro.

Teach Lita How to Generate Memes

Now that you know how to request an image macro from Imgflip's API using Ruby, you can start building out a Lita skill to let chatbot users generate new image macros on command.

Start by generating a new Lita handler:

```
> lita handler imgflip-memes
Do you want to test your plug-in on Travis CI?
  ("yes" or "no", default is "no") yes
Do you want to generate code coverage information with SimpleCov
    and Coveralls.io? ("yes" or "no", default is "no") yes
If your plug-in's Git repository will be hosted on GitHub, build status
    and code coverage badges can be automatically added to your README.
Would you like to add these badges? ("yes" or "no", default is "no") yes
What is your GitHub username? dpritchett
      create  lita-imgflip-memes/lib/lita/handlers/imgflip_memes.rb
      create  lita-imgflip-memes/lib/lita-imgflip-memes.rb
      create  lita-imgflip-memes/spec/lita/handlers/imgflip_memes_spec.rb
      create  lita-imgflip-memes/spec/spec_helper.rb
      create  lita-imgflip-memes/locales/en.yml
      create  lita-imgflip-memes/templates/.gitkeep
      create  lita-imgflip-memes/Gemfile
      create  lita-imgflip-memes/lita-imgflip-memes.gemspec
      create  lita-imgflip-memes/.gitignore
```

---

3. https://www.w3.org/Protocols/rfc2616/rfc2616-sec10.html

```
    create  lita-imgflip-memes/.travis.yml
    create  lita-imgflip-memes/Rakefile
    create  lita-imgflip-memes/README.md
If you plan to release this plug-in as open source software, consider adding
    a LICENSE file to the root of the repository.
Common open source software licenses can be found at
  http://choosealicense.com/.
Remember, for badges to be displayed in your plug-in's README, you must host
    your project on GitHub. Additionally, you will need to configure the
    project on Travis CI and Coveralls.io.
```

As with the other Lita handlers, you elect to include:

- Travis CI build server support for tests on every push to GitHub

- Coveralls code coverage support to track what percentage of the skill's code is tested.

- Build status badges for the README.

- A GitHub username to help RubyGems credit you for your work when the gem is published.

Taking *The Pragmatic Programmer* [4] tracer-bullets approach to making this work—set your sights on a small goal that's representative of a broader intent, make it work, and then build up and out from there—you'll start small.

The following shows a Lita handler that generates an Imgflip image macro URL and prints the results in chat.

lita-imgflip-memes/examples/001_make_meme.rb
```ruby
module Lita
  module Handlers
    class ImgflipMemes < Handler
      Lita.register_handler(self)

      route /^(aliens)\s+(.+)/i, :make_meme, command: true,
        help: 'Aliens guy meme'

      def make_meme(message)
        template_id = 101470
        username = ENV.fetch('IMGFLIP_USERNAME', 'redacted')
        password = ENV.fetch('IMGFLIP_USERNAME', 'redacted')

        # generalize me            ???
        # figure out when i might have multiple matches
        #    instead of just :first
        meme_name, text0, text1 = message.matches.first
```

---

4.   https://pragprog.com/book/tpp20/the-pragmatic-programmer-20th-anniversary-edition

```
      api_url = 'https://api.imgflip.com/caption_image'
      result = http.post api_url, {
        template_id: template_id,
        username: username,
        password: password,
        text0: text0,
        text1: text1
      }
      # clean me up
      image = JSON.parse(result.body).fetch("data").fetch("url")
      message.reply image
    end
   end
  end
end
```

A few things to note about this code:

- There's only one route. A single meme template was selected and its id hard-coded into the :make_meme method.

- The API login information is stored in environment variables; for more about why that's a good idea, see Chapter 3, Deploy Your Lita Bot to Heroku, on page 21.

- There's no error handling. If Lita's network connection fails to reach Imgflip, this code throws an exception.

- The JSON parsing line is particularly dirty with four consecutive method calls, chained together in a naive expectation of continued success.

- The regular expression that watches for input of the form "lita aliens (joke goes here)" is very specific to this particular use case.

- All of the various logical parts of this implementation are crammed into a single large method.

- A multiple assignment unpacks messages.matches.first into three consecutive variables when it receives an array with three strings inside.

- The code continues to lean heavily on the fails-fast-and-loudly fetch method to give quick feedback when digging into the hashmap returned by JSON.parse.

Keeping those earlier ~~shortcomings~~ opportunities for improvement in mind, validate the initial handler implementation in the imgflip_memes_spec.rb file generated by lita handler.

lita-imgflip-memes/examples/002_make_meme_test.rb
```ruby
require "spec_helper"

describe Lita::Handlers::ImgflipMemes, lita_handler: true do
  let(:robot) { Lita::Robot.new(registry) }

  subject { described_class.new(robot) }

  describe 'routes' do
    it { is_expected.to route("Lita aliens chat bots") }
  end

  describe ':make_meme' do
    it 'responds with an image URL' do
      send_message "Lita aliens chat bots"
      expect(replies.last).to match(/http/i)
    end
  end
end
```

In the previous list, you can see that you already have two things right: Lita responds to "Lita aliens chat bots" as expected, and Lita's response looks a lot like a URL.

You may want to dig through the real-time evolution of this Lita handler commit by commit.[5] While this chapter emphasizes the evolution of a working module and the growing pains associated with that growth, the GitHub commit logs show the reality of the trial-and-error and continuous reshaping process. Shaping a good program often feels a lot more like pottery than like Legos.

The next step in this skill's evolution is to extract out a method[6] for the talking-to-Imgflip work. The logic will not change much, but the HTTP call to Imgflip is an excellent candidate to extract into its own method with a unit test.

As you'll see in a moment, the new method takes a template id, a top-line of text, and a bottom-line of text. These three parameters distill the bare minimum variables for defining an image macro using the Imgflip system.

lita-imgflip-memes/examples/003_pull_image.rb
```ruby
def pull_image(template_id, line1, line2)
  username = ENV.fetch('IMGFLIP_USERNAME', 'redacted')
  password = ENV.fetch('IMGFLIP_USERNAME', 'redacted')

  api_url = 'https://api.imgflip.com/caption_image'
  result = http.post api_url, {
    template_id: template_id,
```

---

5.   https://github.com/dpritchett/lita-imgflip-memes/commits/master
6.   https://refactoring.com/catalog/extractMethod.html

```
    username: username,
    password: password,
    text0: line1,
    text1: line2
  }
  # clean me up
  image = JSON.parse(result.body).fetch("data").fetch("url")
end
```

Here are the additions to the spec file.

lita-imgflip-memes/examples/004_pull_image_test.rb
```
# from lita-imgflip-memes/spec/lita/handlers/imgflip_memes_spec.rb
let(:jpeg_url_match) { /http.*\.jpg/i }

describe ':pull_image' do
  it 'returns a jpeg url' do
    aliens_template_id = 101470
    result = subject.pull_image(aliens_template_id, 'hello', 'world')

    expect(result).to match(jpeg_url_match)
  end
end
```

This lets you test the :pull_image method as simply as possible by asserting that you can successfully pass it three well-formed inputs and receive a jpeg URL as a return value.

Expand the Skill to Support More than One Meme

Now that your Lita skill supports one specific meme, you can extend it to support multiple meme templates on demand. For that, you'll build out the capability to register one meme at a time and then access any of them from the chat interface. You'll also update the test suite to demonstrate the new multi-meme capabilities.

Here is the updated handler code:

lita-imgflip-memes/examples/005_add_templates.rb
```
# from lita-imgflip-memes/lib/lita/handlers/imgflip_memes.rb
TEMPLATES = [
  { template_id: 101470, pattern: /^aliens()\s+(.+)/i,
    help: 'Ancient aliens guy' },
  { template_id: 61579, pattern: /(one does not simply) (.+)/i,
    help: 'one does not simply walk into mordor' },
]

TEMPLATES.each do |t|
  route t.fetch(:pattern), :make_meme, command: true, help: t.fetch(:help)
end
```

```ruby
def make_meme(message)
  match = message.matches.first
  raise ArgumentError unless match.size == 2
  line1, line2 = match

  templates = TEMPLATES.select do |t|
    t.fetch(:pattern) == message.pattern
  end
  template = templates.first

  raise ArgumentError if template.nil?

  image = pull_image(template.fetch(:template_id), line1, line2)

  message.reply image
end
```

Note that the TEMPLATES constant provides an implicitly typed hash of meme options, each with its own template id, pattern to match against, and Lita-style help text.

After the TEMPLATES are defined, an each block iterates over them and registers each template's corresponding pattern as a new Lita route. The make_meme method has been updated to start from a matched pattern and then go back to TEMPLATES to figure out which meme template it's asked to work with. In other situations, this might be better served with an actual MemeTemplate class and some hacks to the handler methods, but here, it's more comfortable to stick with the basic idioms of Lita while taking a roundabout path to make it work without having to try to hack Lita directly.

Perhaps the most subtle tweak necessary was the positioning of the regular expression *capture groups* in the pattern: directives. Note that each of the pattern: directives in the preceding 005_add_templates.rb example has two pairs of parentheses. These are intended to extract strings from the user's input to be passed along to the Imgflip API as "top text" and "bottom text." They look like: (), (one does not simply), or (.+). Each of these parentheticals is a regular expression "capture group" that instructs Lita to keep track of the words that it matches for your future use.

If a user types "aliens i have big hair," then the template pattern /^aliens()\s+(.+)/i will match twice: First with an empty string [""]—the captured match for the first parenthetical ()—and again with ["i have big hair"]—the captured match for the second parenthetical (.+). These captured matches are fed into line1 and line2, respectively, in the call to Imgflip. That builds you an image of "i have big hair" with a blank "top text" and a "bottom text."

The empty parentheses say, *I need to capture a string here, but I don't need any text in it for this meme*, which is just right for the bottom-line-only

Ancient Aliens meme. The (.+) says *capture everything from this point forward*, and that's the part you send off as caption line two after triggering on Lita aliens ____.

The One Does Not Simply meme has its own pattern directive. Its first capture group always catches the top text of "One does not simply," while its second capture group catches the actual user input describing what one's not able to simply do. The intent of these regexes can be hard to read; tests help clarify that intent.

With the meme maker extended to conceptually allow for two or more memes, a new test is in order. This one confirms that Lita will respond as expected to the second pattern: one does not simply walk into ____.

lita-imgflip-memes/examples/006_test_two_line_inputs.rb
```
# from lita-imgflip-memes/spec/lita/handlers/imgflip_memes_spec.rb
it 'can handle two-line inputs' do
  send_message 'lita one does not simply walk into mordor'
  expect(replies.last).to match(jpeg_url_match)
end
```

This test verifies that the *one does not simply walk into mordor meme* works as expected. This ensures that both the line1 and line2 supplied to Imgflip are working; you can expect additional meme templates to succeed.

Enable Users to Add Memes to Your Gem

As it stands now, this skill can scale up to arbitrarily large numbers of meme templates with little fuss. However, another layer of complexity is available to you—users of this gem may want to add support for more Imgflip templates than you want to deal with at the moment. This scenario prompts the final refactor: rework the TEMPLATES idiom to allow for programmatic insertion and activation of new meme templates without forcing consumers to open the ImgflipMemes class.

Users of this macro-builder gem will likely want to add new memes, but they won't want to hack into the actual gem to do so. Your goal in this phase is to provide operators of your Imgflip Lita skill with a one-line *add a new meme to the pile* method to this skill. The :add_meme method, which you're about to see, provides a straightforward access point. Here another Sean Bean meme is added, this time with Ned Stark from Game of Thrones. Thanks to the wildcard in this new meme's pattern, Lita will caption a new image whenever a user says something like "brace yourself" or "brace yourselves."

the_bot/lita_config.rb
```
Lita::Handlers::ImgflipMemes.add_meme(
  template_id: 61546,
  pattern: /(brace yoursel[^\s]+) (.*)/i,
  help: 'brace yourselves, <text>')
```

This new add_meme method's signature is nearly identical to the parameters
you used to set up internal memes. A bot operator can paste an add meme call
into the lita_config.rb file of a bot running lita-imgflip-memes and Lita will register
their new meme at boot time.

There are only slight differences in the external versus internal registration
methods. First, operators invoking the add_meme method must specify the full
class name Lita::Handlers::ImgflipMemes, because their code is evaluated in the
context of their host bot's lita_config.rb rather than from within the code of your
Imgflip skill. Second, a new internal :make_meme method allows a consistent
registry of internal versus external memes.

The following imgflip_memes.rb code listings show the final ImgflipMemes handler
alongside explanations of the nuances of each snippet.

lita-imgflip-memes/lib/lita/handlers/imgflip_memes.rb
```
require 'pry'

module Lita
  module Handlers
    class ImgflipMemes < Handler
      class ImgflipApiError < StandardError; end
      class ConnectionError < StandardError; end

      config :api_user, default: ENV['IMGFLIP_API_USER']
      config :api_password, default: ENV['IMGFLIP_API_PASSWORD']

      API_URL = 'https://api.imgflip.com/caption_image'

      @@_templates = []
```

This snippet has several new wrinkles:

- The new error classes ImgflipApiError and ConnectionError are defined in quick
  one-liners to allow for more nuanced reporting of expected failure cases.

- The :config settings allow Lita owners who elect to use this skill to supply
  their API credentials as environment variables (my preference) or use the
  lita_config.rb standard configuration method.

- The API_URL constant pulls this magic string out of the weeds of the
  :make_meme method and gives it pride of place near the top of the file. That's
  a common technique in building API wrapper gems, particularly if the API
  has multiple endpoints that all start with the same root path.

- Last, and most immediately relevant, is the @@_templates = [] declaration. The TEMPLATES constant is gone, replaced with a class variable that exposes an empty array ready to receive new templates as they're submitted via :add_meme. While class variables are best avoided when building classes with future inheritance and composability in mind, they work well enough for this use case.

Here's the old :make_meme method that receives Lita messages, generates memes, and returns image URLs.

lita-imgflip-memes/lib/lita/handlers/imgflip_memes.rb
```ruby
def make_meme(message)
  line1, line2 = extract_meme_text(message.match_data)

  template = find_template(message.pattern)

  begin
    image = pull_image(template.fetch(:template_id), line1, line2)
  rescue ConnectionError, ImgflipApiError => err
    Lita.logger.error(err.message)
    return message.reply 'Bummer - can\'t connect to Imgflip.'
  end

  message.reply image
end
```

New wrinkles include delegation of the relevant meme template lookup to a :find_template method, and a simple begin/rescue/end block around the call to Imgflip's API. If Lita has network issues in hailing Imgflip, it captures the error message, logs it for debugging purposes, and apologizes for the failure in chat.

lita-imgflip-memes/lib/lita/handlers/imgflip_memes.rb
```ruby
def extract_meme_text(match_data)
  _, line1, line2 = match_data.to_a
  return line1, line2
end

def find_template(pattern)
  templates = registered_templates.select do |t|
    t.fetch(:pattern) == pattern
  end
  template = templates.first

  template = registered_templates.select { |t|
    t.fetch(:pattern) == pattern
  }.first
  raise ArgumentError if template.nil?
  return template
end
```

```ruby
def pull_image(template_id, line1, line2)
  username = config.api_user
  password = config.api_password

  begin
    result = http.post API_URL, {
      template_id: template_id,
      username: username,
      password: password,
      text0: line1,
      text1: line2
    }
  rescue Faraday::Error => err
    raise ConnectionError, err.message
  end

  # clean me up
  parsed = JSON.parse(result.body)

  if parsed.keys.include?('error_message')
    raise(ImgflipApiError, parsed['error_message'])
  end

  parsed.fetch('data', {}).fetch('url')
end
```

The :extract_meme_text method here is a streamlined version of the same functionality in past iterations:

- MatchData is a Ruby standard library class that packages up the results of a regular expression match. The first bit of the :match_data array is the full text that was matched against—that is ignored by assigning it to an unused variable named _. The next two matches are stored as line1 and line2 because they are actually needed.

- The find template method works as before, but it looks in a new location named registered_templates, which is ultimately backed by the @@_templates variable seen earlier.

- The pull image method receives the three required pieces of information for an Imgflip call, makes a POST request, and catches any Faraday errors that come up from a failure to POST.

- :pull_image next parses the received JSON payload, checks for an Imgflip-generated error_message key, and handles that.

- When all error handling is taken care of, :pull_image returns the expected image URL, completing the 'happy path'.

Next is an add meme class method:

```ruby
    def self.add_meme(template_id:, pattern:, help:)
      @@_templates << { template_id: template_id, pattern: pattern,
                        help: help }
      if parsed.keys.include?('error_message')
        raise(ImgflipApiError, parsed['error_message'])
      end
      image = parsed.fetch('data', {}).fetch('url')
    end

    def self.add_meme(template_id:, pattern:, help:)
      @@_templates << {
        template_id: template_id, pattern: pattern, help: help
      }

      route pattern, :make_meme, help: help
    end

    def registered_templates
      self.class.registered_templates
    end

    def self.registered_templates
      @@_templates
    end

    add_meme(template_id: 101470, pattern: /^aliens()\s+(.+)/i,
             help: {
               'aliens invisible sandwich' => 'Ancient Aliens Guy meme'
             })
    add_meme(template_id: 61579, pattern: /(one does not simply) (.*)/i,
             help: {
               'one does not simply walk into mordor' => 'Boromir meme'
             })

    Lita.register_handler(self)
  end
 end
end
```

These are the last bits of infrastructure propping up the user-friendly :add_meme refactoring. The add meme method itself creates a new hashmap with the expected keys and values and appends the hashmap to the shared @@_templates class variable. A pair of :registered_templates instance-level and class-level methods allow for read-only access to the memes injected by :add_meme. At the very end are two calls to :add_meme that verify the original Alien Guy, and that the One Does Not Simply memes still work under the newly complicated meme registry architecture.

With all of this refactoring and new functionality, some new tests are in order.

The following is a test of the :extract_meme_text functionality that verifies that the TEMPLATES to @@_templates refactor was successful.

```
lita-imgflip-memes/spec/lita/handlers/imgflip_memes_spec.rb
describe ':extract_meme_text' do
  let(:matchers) { described_class.registered_templates }

  it 'can properly match no-first-line inputs' do
    matcher = matchers.select { |t| t.fetch(:template_id) == 101470 }.first
    pattern = matcher.fetch(:pattern)

    match_data = pattern.match 'aliens chat bots'
    result = subject.extract_meme_text match_data

    expect(result).to eql(['', 'chat bots'])
  end

  it 'can properly capture meme text that is part of the trigger' do
    matcher = matchers.select { |t| t.fetch(:template_id) == 61579 }.first
    pattern = matcher.fetch(:pattern)

    match_data = pattern.match 'one does not simply walk into mordor'
    result = subject.extract_meme_text match_data

    expect(result).to eql(['one does not simply', 'walk into mordor'])
  end
end
```

The *can properly capture meme text* bit at the bottom is what triggered the need for a move to MatchData-based template introspection.

Lita's test helpers let you test that an input is routed to a specific method and also that a specific input produces a specific output, but they didn't seem interested in helping to dig into the details of the object Lita passes to a handler function (i.e., :make_meme) when a route is triggered. By digging around with pry and recognizing that the object passed to :make_meme leveraged the standard MatchData class, you can rearrange the tests to operate on a simple MatchData object rather than trying to simulate a full Lita response handling code path.

Wrap-up

With that, the Imgflip meme maker skill is more than capable for single-channel meme generation needs. In the course of growing this skill from a tracer bullet prototype to a tested, extensible gem implementation, you have covered many of the common aspects of the care and feeding of Lita bots. You exercised some regular expression techniques that can enable a broad spectrum of input handling needs. You also learned how to make your Lita skills extensible to future consumers of your gem so they can get more leverage out of the tools you deliver.

In the next chapter, you learn how to make Lita extensions that impact the bot's fundamental performance beyond the single-skill level, including how to schedule Lita housekeeping tasks. After that, you'll learn multiple methods for changing Lita's input and output styles: catch-all responders and techniques for dealing with too-long responses.

Challenges

- You've just learned how to add pre-existing Imgflip meme templates to your Lita bot. Go browse Imgflip's meme catalog[7] and find five templates worth adding to your community's Lita bot.

- Imgflip's caption_image API offers additional customization options[8] beyond specifying the top and bottom text. Try to enable your users to specify the color of their generated meme text. Try letting them adjust the positioning or font size.

- Imgflip's meme catalog welcomes submissions. Find a photo or illustration that is meaningful to your Lita bot's audience and add it as a new Imgflip template that Lita can use!

---

7. https://imgflip.com/memesearch?q=meme
8. https://api.imgflip.com/

## CHAPTER 8

Bot Task Scheduler

There are times when you need to crack open Lita's internals and change some core behavior. In this chapter, you'll serialize a user's Lita command as a plain Ruby hash and then replay that serialized command through Lita in the future. You'll also use Lita's built-in Redis persistence layer to manage the schedule itself.

The skill you'll build in this chapter is a complex chatbot integration that allows you to defer any of your other Lita skills with a work scheduler.

Capture a Lita Command to Reuse Later

To capture a Lita command, you need to stub out three routes. The main route captures a message, while the other two manage the scheduled messages, one to show the list and the other to empty it out.

lita-task-scheduler/lib/lita/handlers/task_scheduler.rb
```
route(/^schedule\s+"(.+)"\s+in\s+(.+)$/i, :schedule_command, command: true)
route(/^show schedule$/i, :show_schedule, command: true)
route(/^empty schedule$/i, :empty_schedule, command: true)
```

The expected use for each of the three routes is as follows:

```
> Lita schedule "double 2" in 5 seconds
> Lita show schedule
> Lita empty schedule
```

The first route uses a regular expression to capture all of the text between a pair of quotes: "(.+)"; this is the command Lita stores to reissue in the future. A second capture in the same regular expression represents the time when the command is expected to be reissued. The other two routes are plain commands that don't require the capture of any metadata, which makes them comparatively easier to capture.

Confirm that each of these three routes matches as expected with some routing specs:

lita-task-scheduler/spec/lita/handlers/task_scheduler_spec.rb
```
describe 'routing' do
  it { is_expected.to route('Lita schedule "double 4" in 2 hours') }
  it { is_expected.to route('Lita show schedule') }
  it { is_expected.to route('Lita empty schedule') }
end
```

Be aware, the schedule route is likely to feel brittle to your end users—not everyone will remember the "lita schedule (double quotes here) (delayed command here) (another double quote)" syntax. But you can keep an eye out for common command failures to see whether you can bake those in as alternative routes. Discoverability and the principle of least astonishment[1] are key to an enjoyable chatbot user experience.

Extract content from an incoming message

The next two sections are rather messy because they require you to crack open a Lita Message object, pull out its key elements, and keep them on ice until you're ready to rebuild a new Message that smells and tastes like the original. Since quite a bit of code is required to stitch all of this together, you'll see only the key methods in this chapter. The full implementation is available in the lita-bot-task-scheduler folder in the source code listings that ship with this book.

In the meantime, start with the following method for scheduling commands.

lita-task-scheduler/lib/lita/handlers/task_scheduler.rb
```
def schedule_command(payload)
  task, timing = payload.matches.last
  run_at = parse_timing(timing)
  serialized = command_to_hash(payload.message, new_body: task)

  defer_task(serialized, run_at)
  show_schedule payload
end
```

This method takes an incoming Lita command with a :schedule_command method and parses the user's command into a task—the thing you want to do—and a timing—when you want to do it, represented by how far in the future you want Lita to perform this task. The timing interpretation parse_timing method, and the storage of the user's intent as a resubmittable command, are managed by command_to_hash.

---

1. https://en.wikipedia.org/wiki/Principle_of_least_astonishment

The parse_timing logic is purposefully simplistic.

```
lita-task-scheduler/lib/lita/handlers/task_scheduler.rb
def parse_timing(timing)
  count, unit = timing.split
  count = count.to_i
  unit = unit.downcase.strip.gsub(/s$/, '')

  seconds = case unit
            when 'second'
              count
            when 'minute'
              count * 60
            when 'hour'
              count * 60 * 60
            when 'day'
              count * 60 * 60 * 24
            else
              raise ArgumentError, "I don't recognize #{unit}"
            end

  Time.now.utc + seconds
end
```

You take in a string that looks like "5 seconds" or "3 days" and you reduce it to a specific number of seconds from now. The return value is the computed UTC time when your task is expected to execute. Storing timestamps in UTC is handy when you're building logic around timestamps retrieved from a database. If you don't specify UTC, you may find that your database assumes everything is in its local time (say, Chicago time), while your application is running on a server that's set to a different time zone. Things get hairy pretty quickly when your application thinks a timestamp means one thing, but the database stores it as something else—retrieving a record later can end up with an unwanted time offset sneaking in on you.

The time parsing tests are a little easier to read than the implementation—you assert that the future time computed by inputs like "2 weeks" and "1 day" are within a fraction of a second's tolerance of the timestamp you'd expect them to be.

Capture Lita's Message object intent for reuse

The next method captures and stores the essence of a Lita Message object for reuse.

```
lita-task-scheduler/lib/lita/handlers/task_scheduler.rb
def command_to_hash(command, new_body: nil)
  {
    user_name: command.user.name,
    room_name: command.source.room,
    body: new_body || command.body
  }
end
```

Note that the command parameter is the original Message object captured by the scheduler route. The goal is to figure out who sent this, in which channel, and what exactly they wanted it to do.

The new_body parameter allows you to keep only the interesting part of a scheduled task command—the actual task itself—and not the scheduling metadata: schedule "double 2" in 5 seconds becomes double 2.

Send an extracted task to your scheduler

The serialized command intent is now ready to be shipped off to Lita's Redis datastore for future reuse.

Here's the defer_task method your handler depends on to store this intent:

```
lita-task-scheduler/lib/lita/handlers/task_scheduler.rb
def defer_task(serialized_task, run_at)
  scheduler.add(serialized_task, run_at)
end
```

And here are some specs to outline what's expected from the last few methods:

```
lita-task-scheduler/spec/lita/handlers/task_scheduler_spec.rb
describe ':defer_task' do
  it 'defers any single task' do
    message = { canary_message: Time.now }
    run_at = Time.now + 5
    result = subject.defer_task(message, run_at)
    expect(result).to include(message)
  end

  it 'stores multiple same-second tasks in an array' do
    message = { 'canary_message' => Time.now.to_i }
    run_at = Time.now + 5

    5.times do
      subject.defer_task(message, run_at)
    end

    result = subject.defer_task(message, run_at)

    expect(result).to eq([message] * 6)
  end
end
```

The actual Redis-wrapping code for storing and retrieving these schedules is in the final section of this chapter. Skip ahead if you're curious.

Resubmit a Deferred Lita Command

Excellent, the scene is set. The user issues a Lita command to run a few minutes or hours from now, and that command is safely tucked away in Redis. Now, you'll want to keep an eye on the schedule to pull out tasks as they're ready. You can do this with a schedule-checking loop that ticks once a second.

Tick through a schedule checking loop

The run_loop method, shown next, is wired up by Lita at boot time using the :loaded event.

```
lita-task-scheduler/lib/lita/handlers/task_scheduler.rb
def run_loop
  Thread.new do
    loop do
      tick
      sleep 1
    end
  end
end

def tick
  tasks = find_tasks_due
  tasks.each { |t| resend_command t }
  Lita.logger.debug "Task loop done for #{Time.now}"
end

on(:loaded) { run_loop }
```

"On loaded" sends off your run_loop method to a new background thread so that Lita can listen to user input immediately; the scheduler would otherwise block the main thread and render the bot unusable. The tick method calls out to the scheduler object to see whether any tasks are due right now or in the immediate past. Any tasks it finds are sent on to the resend_command method.

You can use a test to confirm that the tick method resends any eligible tasks it discovers.

```
lita-task-scheduler/spec/lita/handlers/task_scheduler_spec.rb
describe 'tick' do
  before { subject.stub(:find_tasks_due).and_return ['a_task'] }
```

```
  it 'should find tasks due and resend them' do
    expect(subject).to receive(:find_tasks_due)
    expect(subject).to receive(:resend_command).with('a_task')

    subject.tick
  end
end
```

Resend a command to execute now

The resend command method cracks into Lita's innards more than is usual for this book.

```
lita-task-scheduler/lib/lita/handlers/task_scheduler.rb
def resend_command(command_hash)
  user = Lita::User.new(command_hash.fetch('user_name'))
  room = Lita::Room.new(command_hash.fetch('room_name'))
  source = Lita::Source.new(user: user, room: room)
  body = "#{robot.name} #{command_hash.fetch('body')}"

  newmsg = Lita::Message.new(
    robot,
    body,
    source
  )

  robot.receive newmsg
end
```

You already know the originating user and source channel for the required task. Creating new User, Room, and Source objects lets Lita prepare to resend the message as if it were brand new. The robot.receive command accepts the newly recreated message, and Lita executes the command immediately.

In the next section, you'll double back to revisit the Scheduler object, which has been hiding most of the complexity of the Redis integration and your schedule data structures until now.

Store Scheduled Tasks in Redis

This module crystallizes the core requirements of the scheduler:

- Add a specific task to the schedule datastore with a specific future timestamp, for example, "double 2," "in 4 minutes."

- Check the schedule datastore to see whether any tasks have past-due timestamps.

You need to set the stage for storing tasks with a new Lita::Scheduler class that announces its intent to work with a specific Redis hash data structure stored in a location with a relevant name.

```
lita-task-scheduler/lib/lita/scheduler.rb
module Lita
  class Scheduler
    REDIS_TASKS_KEY = name.to_s

    def initialize(redis:, logger:)
      @redis = redis
      @logger = logger
    end

    attr_reader :redis, :logger

    def get_all
      redis.hgetall(REDIS_TASKS_KEY)
    end
```

Note the auto-generated hash key name for storing everything in a single Redis hash. The get_all call simply wraps up the task scheduler skill's need to list absolutely everything for schedule reporting purposes.

Store a new schedule item in Redis

To store a schedule item, you need to design a data structure suitable for holding lists of scheduled tasks, ordered by timestamp. The plan is to use a hash object using integer timestamps as keys. Each timestamp's values will be arrays of serialized messages.

Here's a sketch of a single command being stored in Redis:

```
> lita schedule "double 2" in 2 seconds
```

That command can be represented as follows:

```
> example_command = {
    user: 'author',
    room: 'example',
    command: 'double 2'
  }
```

This is the only command you're scheduling to run two seconds from now, so you store it inside an array with a single member—this serialized command.

The current time can be represented as the number of seconds since the Unix epoch[2] on January 1st, 1970:

```
> key_time = Time.now.to_i + 2
1523926393
```

---

2. https://en.wikipedia.org/wiki/Unix_time

Two seconds from now is 1523926393 in Unix time. This gives you everything you need to store the schedule for that particular second in Redis:

```
redis.hset(REDIS_TASKS_KEY, key_time.to_s, [example_command])
```

At this point, your task's key hash in Redis looks like this:

```
{
    "1523926393" => [
        {
            user: 'author',
            room: 'example',
            command: 'double 2'
        }
    ]
}
```

Now, look at the Scheduler#add method:

lita-task-scheduler/lib/lita/scheduler.rb
```
def add(payload, timestamp)
  key_time = timestamp.to_i.to_s

  redis.watch(REDIS_TASKS_KEY)

  tasks = redis.hget(REDIS_TASKS_KEY, key_time) || []

  tasks = JSON.parse(tasks) unless tasks.empty?
  tasks << payload

  redis.hset(REDIS_TASKS_KEY, key_time, tasks.to_json)

  redis.unwatch
  tasks
end
```

Not only does it use hset to push a new task onto the reserved Redis hash, but it also takes care of the mess of maintaining more than one task per second.

Pull past-due tasks from the schedule to be executed

With tasks properly storing in Redis under their expected timestamps, all that's left for you to do with this skill is to extract tasks as they come due for resubmitting to Lita as chat commands.

lita-task-scheduler/lib/lita/scheduler.rb
```
def find_tasks_due
  results = []
  timestamps = redis.hkeys(REDIS_TASKS_KEY)

  timestamps.each do |t|
    key_time = Time.at(t.to_i)
    next unless key_time <= Time.now
```

```
    tasks_raw = redis.hget(REDIS_TASKS_KEY, t)
    tasks = JSON.parse(tasks_raw)

    results += tasks
    redis.hdel(REDIS_TASKS_KEY, t)
  end

  results
end
```

The find_tasks_due command iterates over all of the timestamp keys it finds in the schedule and then looks closer at the ones that are in the past. Any timestamp from the past is assumed to be a task list that needs to be run right now and is set aside to be returned at the end of the method. All processed task lists are quickly deleted from Redis, so they won't show up when the scheduler comes back the next second.

Testing the find_tasks_due functionality is a matter of probing the boundaries.

lita-task-scheduler/spec/lita/handlers/task_scheduler_spec.rb
```
describe ':find_tasks_due' do
  context 'two tasks are scheduled for five seconds ago' do
    before { 2.times { subject.defer_task('past_task', Time.now - 5) } }

    it 'returns all past due tasks' do
      result = subject.find_tasks_due
      expected = %w[past_task past_task]
      expect(result).to eq(expected)
    end
  end

  context 'one task scheduled in the future' do
    before { subject.defer_task('future_task', Time.now + 100) }

    it 'does not return that new task' do
      result = subject.find_tasks_due
      expect(result).to_not include('future_task')
    end
  end
end
```

So, what happens when a couple of tasks are stored with a timestamp in the recent past? They should show up on the next find_tasks_due call. What about a task in the near future; will it show up? No, it shouldn't show up—at least not yet.

Your end-to-end task capturing, scheduling, and running is now complete. A quick test using the doubler skill should confirm it:

```
BookBot > bookbot schedule "double 4" in 5 seconds
Scheduled tasks:
 - "double 4" at 2018-04-16 07:39:39 -0500
BookBot > 4 + 4 = 8
```

Wrap-up

In this chapter, you gained a little insight as to how some of Lita's core classes are put together. This knowledge is helpful when you need to crack open Lita's internals and change some core behavior.

In the next chapter, you'll integrate a response shortening service. With this service, you can gracefully handle text responses that might fill the whole screen in a typical Lita-enabled chat room. This comes in handy when implementing informational lookups like dictionaries or Wikipedia. Not everyone needs to see paragraph two of your Urban Dictionary definition.

Challenges

- The timing for your scheduler is all relative. Try parsing and scheduling against specific future times like, "Monday the 4th at 8 a.m."

- The schedule reporter does not separate schedules on a per-user basis. See whether you can add that in.

- Deleting individual schedules by index ("lita delete schedule 1") would be more useful than wiping all of them. How can you make that happen?

- The scheduling information is stored in a sort of ad hoc data structure in Redis. Try formalizing this into some classes or structs to firm up the data interchange and limit future bugs.

- The test file for the Scheduler doesn't really test the scheduler functionality in isolation—all calls are passed through the Lita handler. Can you separate these concerns so the Scheduler is portable for other use cases?

## CHAPTER 9

Hide Walls of Text Behind an Offsite URL

Response hygiene is an important tool for preserving your community's good vibes toward their bots and botmakers. And it's common for chatbot operators to want to integrate with offsite knowledge bases like Wikipedia, the Internet Movie Database, and the Urban Dictionary (well, maybe not that last one). As useful as these references are, the text responses tend to span multiple paragraphs; this is likely to irritate many folks in your chat room who aren't interested in reading thousands of words about someone's favorite rock, for example.

In this chapter, you'll build and integrate a Lita extension that provides consistent ways for you to modify outputs before the replies are sent to your chat rooms. You'll still deliver relevant content, but you'll spare your users a wall of text by redirecting long responses through an offsite text snippet hosting service, like Pastebin or GitHub's Gists.

You'll turn an ugly interaction like this one:

```
> Lita what are the first ten billion words on the internet
... lita begins responding,
... eventually gets banned or breaks your chat server :(
```

into a gentler, more hygienic interaction like this:

```
> Lita what are the first ten billion words on the internet
The first ten billion words on the internet are https://pastebin.com/9k82HWCY
```

The second response is much gentler and less distracting. Not to mention, it doesn't break your chat room.

Responses like the latter became necessary when the IRC Hubot started learning skills with unreasonably long replies. The biggest offender was the help command, which scaled linearly with the number of skills added. Long story short: a way was found to redirect the offending long-text response to an API (pastebin or gist) that lets you hide the wall of text behind a URL instead of cluttering up the room. This is good, because the alternative was getting kicked by the network for flooding—or even worse, was irritating the chatbot's constituency.

Create a Lita Extension to Send Text to the Pastebin API

Pastebin is a service that provides two main uses: First, it provides a public space to store a text dump at a permanent URL. Maybe you're storing a code snippet or some meeting minutes? Second, it auto-expires those notes after a scheduled period, say 24 hours. It can be a relief to share some scratch notes and know that they'll be purged over time. These twin purposes are ideal for screening out a too-long post from your chat room.

Following is the ShipToPastebin implementation in its entirety; you'll note that it's a very short file. All the extension aims to do is expose a method—for use by proper Lita skills—that receives a long string and returns a Pastebin URL. To create your new extension, you'll type lita extension ship-to-pastebin at the console. Once it creates your extension, type the following into the ship_to_pastebin.rb file:

```ruby
lita-ship-to-pastebin/lib/lita/extensions/ship_to_pastebin.rb
require 'faraday'

module Lita
  module Extensions
    class ShipToPastebin
      API_KEY_DEFAULT = 'd88582e90ba06b60569dc55ab5b678ce'

      PASTEBIN_URL = 'https://pastebin.com/api/api_post.php'.freeze

      PasteBinError = Class.new(StandardError)

      def save_to_pastebin(message, title: "Lita's Wall of Text",
                           api_key: API_KEY_DEFAULT )
        begin
          result = Faraday.post PASTEBIN_URL, {
            api_dev_key: api_key,
            api_paste_name: title,
            api_paste_code: message,
            api_paste_expire_date: '1D', # delete after a day
            api_option: 'paste'
          }
        rescue Faraday::Error => err
          raise ConnectionError, err.message
        end
```

```ruby
      if !result.success? || result.body.include?('Bad API')
        raise PasteBinError,
          "Unable to deal with this Faraday response: [#{result.body}]"
      end

      result.body
    end
  end
 end
end
```

Since this extension has exactly one purpose, the direct test is straightforward. You'll create a string, send it off to Pastebin, and then verify that Pastebin returns a URL—presumably the URL for a page containing your long text response.

lita-ship-to-pastebin/spec/lita/extensions/ship_to_pastebin_spec.rb
```ruby
require 'spec_helper'

describe Lita::Extensions::ShipToPastebin, lita: true do
  subject { Lita::Extensions::ShipToPastebin.new }

  # thanks webmock!
  before { stub_pastebin_calls! }

  it 'saves text to pastebin' do
    actual = subject.save_to_pastebin 'hey john', title: 'hey there john'

    # e.g. https://pastebin.com/Vi4Cgn6i
    expect(actual).to match(%r{^https:\/\/pastebin\.com\/[a-zA-Z0-9]+})
  end
end
```

This test setup has to leverage webmock to stop sending real Pastebin API requests every time you run the suite. Pastebin's API rate limits aren't high enough to waste your quota on tests. Webmock works by intercepting outbound HTTP calls—like the ones you're making to Pastebin—and returning pre-configured dummy values. This lets you test whether Pastebin was called without actually bugging Pastebin. You'll first need to add Webmock to your gemspec file, and then you'll need to run bundle to get it downloaded.

lita-ship-to-pastebin/lita-ship-to-pastebin.gemspec
```ruby
spec.add_development_dependency 'webmock', '~> 3.3'
```

The next step is to integrate Webmock with your test harness by requiring it in spec_helper. From there, you need to write up your own "stub out the HTTP requests in this section" convenience method.

```
lita-ship-to-pastebin/spec/spec_helper.rb
require 'webmock/rspec'

# call me in a before block anywhere you're calling pastebin!
#    This will save you from fairly low-overhead API limits.
def stub_pastebin_calls!
  stub_request(:post, 'https://pastebin.com/api/api_post.php')
    .with(body: {
      'api_dev_key' => /[a-f0-9]+/,
      'api_option' => 'paste',
      'api_paste_expire_date' => '1D',
      'api_paste_code' => /\W+/,
      'api_paste_name' => /\W+/ },
    headers: {
      'Accept' => '*/*',
      'Accept-Encoding' => 'gzip;q=1.0,deflate;q=0.6,identity;q=0.3',
      'Content-Type' => 'application/x-www-form-urlencoded',
      'User-Agent' => 'Faraday v0.15.0'
    })
    .to_return(
      status: 200,
      body: 'https://pastebin.com/6ig4DLUQ',
      headers: {}
    )
end
```

Here's what you need to know about that stub_pastebin_calls! method:

First, it's defined in the spec_helper file, which is included in all of your regular spec files, so you can call it at any point from any of those files. The usage pattern follows a three-part "stub this // with that // and return the other" formula. In this case, you're using it to stub out any POSTs to the Pastebin API URL. The with block lists a catch-all pattern of POST body and header info just broad enough to allow Webmock to intercept any of the calls you make to Pastebin. Lastly the "to return" section specifies a dummy return value for any intercepted Pastebin POSTs. You'll fold this stub block into your specs so that you know how to positively test for a "yes, pastebin did what we expected" scenario.

Don't worry about creating those complex-looking Webmock with patterns off the top of your head; you won't have to do that. WebMock will throw a Web-Mock::NetConnectNotAllowedError with a preconfigured stub_request, .with(), and .and_return() block any time you make a request from your test suite, but Web-mock wasn't expecting it.

Make a Simple Lita Handler Skill to Use as a Test Driver

The ship-to-pastebin extension appears to work as tested, but you'll want to integrate it with a Lita handler skill to make sure its interface is appropriate for regular Lita work. To that end, there's an entire sample Lita skill in the code/lita-ship-to-pastebin folder that comes with this book named Bigtext. Bigtext is an only-useful-for-teaching-purposes skill that randomly generates long strings of words and pastes them into your chatroom. This is the perfect test bed to prove the value of the hide-it-in-Pastebin approach. Think of it as Lorem Ipsum for Lita skill testing.

Since Bigtext is merely a demonstration skill with little value as a standalone skill, you can skip the lita handler bigtext ritual and hand-roll the following three files for your ShipToPastebin test suite:

- lib/lita-bigtext.rb is boilerplate that enables autoloading of the Bigtext class.
- lib/lita/handlers/bigtext.rb is the simple implementation of this dummy skill.
- spec/lita/handlers/bigtext_spec.rb tests the dummy skill including its integration with your Pastebin extension.

The following snippet shows the autoloading magic behind every Lita class, including the Bigtext gem. In other chapters, you won't worry about changing these because they aren't hiding multiple Lita modules in a single repository. This Bigtext mini-module exists only in the lib/lita/handlers folder of your lita-ship-to-pastebin module. It technically works like any other Lita handler for the purpose of testing your Pastebin integration, but it skipped all of the RubyGem boilerplate you need or want for a standalone skill.

```
lita-ship-to-pastebin/lib/lita-bigtext.rb
require "lita"

Lita.load_locales Dir[File.expand_path(
  File.join("..", "..", "locales", "*.yml"), __FILE__
)]

require "lita/handlers/bigtext"

Lita::Handlers::Bigtext.template_root File.expand_path(
  File.join("..", "..", "templates"),
  __FILE__
)
```

The Bigtext handler itself generates hundred-word strings with a :longtext method. Since these are unwieldy in a chat scenario, your use of the :hide_bigtext chat route will launder the :longtext through ShipToPastebin. That enables :hide_bigtext to reply with a Pastebin URL instead of the original big text.

lita-ship-to-pastebin/lib/lita/handlers/bigtext.rb

```ruby
route(/^bigtext/i,
      :hide_bigtext,
      command: true,
      help: {
        'bigtext' => 'gimme a wall of text hidden behind a pastebin URL'
      })

def hide_bigtext(message)
  too_long = longtext
  url_placeholder = snip_text too_long
  message.reply url_placeholder
end

def snip_text(text)
  Lita::Extensions::ShipToPastebin.new.
    save_to_pastebin(text, api_key: config.pastebin_api_key)
end

def longtext
  (1..100).each.map do
    %w[able baker charlie delta echo alpha bravo hawaii].sample
  end.join(' ')
end
```

Testing Bigtext looks like any other handler's specs. In this case, you copy in the regular expression used to validate your Pastebin extension's results and confirm that the Bigtext responses match the same profile.

You can use stub_pastebin_calls! from your spec_helper to avoid wasted calls to Pastebin each time you rerun your test suite. Your API access quota would not put up with that forever!

lita-ship-to-pastebin/spec/lita/handlers/bigtext_spec.rb

```ruby
require 'spec_helper'

describe Lita::Handlers::Bigtext, lita_handler: true do
  let(:robot) { Lita::Robot.new(registry) }
  let(:response) { double('response') }

  before { stub_pastebin_calls! }

  context 'managing walls of text' do
    let(:longtext) { subject.longtext }

    it 'should generate a lot of words on demand' do
      expect(longtext.length > 512).to be_truthy
    end
```

```ruby
  it 'should leverage the pastebin extension' do
    result = subject.snip_text(longtext)

    # only one phrase, not 100 words
    expect(result.split.length > 10).to be_falsey

    # stubbing out Faraday calls to hide from Pastebin API limits
    expect(result).to(
      match(%r{^https:\/\/pastebin\.com\/[a-zA-Z0-9]+})
    )
  end

  it 'should use pastebin extension when responding to users' do
    send_message 'Lita bigtext'
    expect(replies.last).to(
      match(%r{^https:\/\/pastebin\.com\/[a-zA-Z0-9]+})
    )
  end
  end
end
```

The expected interaction with Bigtext looks like this:

lita-ship-to-pastebin/examples/000-bigtext-in-action.session
```
$ bundle exec lita
lita Type "exit" or "quit" to end the session.
Lita > lita bigtext
https://pastebin.com/9k82HWCY
Lita >

# adding the /raw/ to the URL so we can see the plain text
$ curl https://pastebin.com/raw/9k82HWCY
bravo hawaii alpha echo charlie baker hawaii delta able echo hawaii baker
echo able baker alpha charlie charlie hawaii charlie delta hawaii alpha
charlie hawaii hawaii hawaii echo hawaii able able charlie delta delta
hawaii echo delta able alpha hawaii delta echo echo charlie bravo bravo
able echo alpha echo baker bravo able able alpha hawaii charlie alpha
hawaii alpha baker delta able delta able delta alpha hawaii hawaii baker
able hawaii echo echo able delta charlie delta echo alpha alpha bravo
bravo charlie echo able able able delta delta hawaii charlie bravo bravo
alpha delta echo able echo echo⏎
```

Note that you'd need to regenerate Bigtext into a standalone skill with the full complement of files if you want to play with it in a live Lita session. To do that, run lita handler new bigtext and then copy in the Bigtext source from this chapter. Clicking through on your new Pastebin URL opens a temporary page full of some freshly generated "able baker alpha bravo charlie." By design, these Pastebin URLs will expire within a few days (shown in the screenshots on page 106).

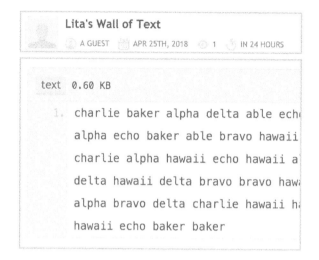

Wrap-up

This chapter has given you another API integration to use with your Lita bots. It's also given you your first example of a Lita extension to add to your handlers. This extension is at its core some Lita-agnostic Ruby code, but you did use Faraday and the Lita test harness, so it fits in pretty well with the overall set of Lita skills you're building up. The example of building a throwaway Bigtext Lita skill inside this extension's codebase should be a useful tool for you in future projects.

In the next chapter, you learn two techniques for generating nearly human responses for your chatbot so that Lita can answer any unexpected inputs with some English jabber of her own. This isn't incredibly useful, but it's proven to be an engaging chatbot technique. The first is a Markov chain generator that allows your bot to mimic the "voice" of a body of text that you train her on, such as Melville's *Moby Dick*. The second technique integrates a rather more complex artificial intelligence named Cleverbot, which has its own API for general use.

Challenges

- Pastebin's API provides several other customization options beyond your basic "body of message goes here." Browse the official API feature documentation[1] to see whether you can add another tweak to your pastebins. Maybe your pastes could use titles ("paste name") or a user-specified expiration date.

---

1. https://pastebin.com/api.php

- Pastebin is a decent place to share code snippets. Now that you're officially a Ruby programmer, try setting up a second Pastebin-related Lita chat route that uses Pastebin's `api_paste_format` option to submit Ruby code through chat and have Pastebin properly format the results.

- Pastebin provides a search facility to find snippets including specified keywords. Using the skills you honed in the Meetup chapter, you might be able to build out a Pastebin search right in your Lita bot.

## CHAPTER 10

Use a Markov Chain or Cleverbot

In this chapter, you'll build two Lita skills that generate nearly human responses. The first of these skills leverages a Markov chain to generate nearly intelligible gibberish whenever your bot hears a question for which it does not have an answer. The second skill uses a somewhat more sophisticated conversational AI named Cleverbot and shares Cleverbot's responses with your chat users.

Markov Chain: Train Lita to Speak in Someone Else's Voice

In this section, you'll use a Markov chain to respond to users' questions. Markov chains are a technique for probabilistically generating content based on observations of past content. In a chatbot context, that means feeding a large corpus—lots and lots of words, such as a book or a collection of emails—into an analyzer and observing which words and phrases are most likely to come after any given word. As a small example, consider the following two sentences:

The cow jumped over the moon.

The quick brown fox jumped over the lazy dog.

If you were trying to implement a naive predictive text generator using only those two sentences as inputs, you could see that the word "jumped" is followed by the word "over" 100% of the time. Keeping that in mind, ask a hypothetical Markov chain service to generate a follow-on word to "jumped":

```
> SuperSimpleMarkov.train 'The cow jumped over the moon'
  true
> SuperSimpleMarkov.train 'The quick brown fox jumped over the lazy dog'
  true

> SuperSimpleMarkov.predict 'jumped'
  [['over', 1.0]] # 100% weight for the word predicted to follow 'jumped'
```

```
  # 25% weight for each of the four words predicted to follow 'the'
> SuperSimpleMarkov.predict 'the'
  [['cow', 0.25], ['moon', 0.25], ['quick', 0.25], ['lazy', 0.25]]

> SuperSimpleMarkov.predict 'over'
  ['the', 1.0]

> SuperSimpleMarkov.generate 'jumped'
  'over'

> 3.times { puts SuperSimpleMarkov.generate 'the' }
  'quick'
  'moon'
  'moon'
```

This example is purposefully simple to demonstrate the core principle of predictive text underlying the Markov chain generator you're going to set up. With that tiny training corpus, there are four possible follow-on words after the word "the," each with an equal 25% chance of appearance. The word "jumped" will always be followed by the word "over"; its list of predicted follow-ons contains only a single word with a 100% weight.

The deeper techniques underlying a proper Markov chain generator are outside the scope of this book, so in the next section, you'll prop one up using the MarkyMarkov gem, and you'll integrate it with Lita.

The process begins by creating a Markov brain and instrumenting it to allow Lita to feed it a corpus of text on demand. After that's in place, you'll create a new Lita handler that responds to unexpected inputs with Markov-generated gibberish.

Create a Markov brain

Your Markov brain can work in isolation outside of a Lita context, but for the purposes of this book, you'll build it as a separate class inside a Lita handler skill. You'll create the empty shell of your Lita skill, fill in a MarkovBrain class, and then build up the actual Lita handler around it.

Start by creating a new Lita handler skill at your shell:

```
$ lita handler markov-blabber
```

Switch into the newly generated lita-markov-blabber folder and type up a new dependency on the marky_markov gem:

```
spec.add_runtime_dependency 'marky_markov', '~> 0.3.5'`
```

With this dependency registered, type bundle to download your new handler's dependencies. When they are downloaded, you can start building a Markov brain.

Here's a look at the public interface of the Markov brain:

```
lita-markov-blabber/lib/lita/markov_brain.rb
# include the markov gem to provide our core functionality
require 'marky_markov'

class Lita::MarkovBrain
  # define a custom error class for easier debugging
  NoBrainInputsFound = Class.new(StandardError)

  # build and load a new in-memory brain from the input text.
  #   inputs_path is a *required* input
  def initialize(inputs_path:)
    @inputs_path = File.absolute_path(inputs_path)
    @dictionary = ::MarkyMarkov::TemporaryDictionary.new
    load_brain!
  end

  # given a number N, return a string with N words
  def generate_n_words(n)
    dictionary.generate_n_words(n)
  end
```

MarkovBrain begins with the declaration of a special error class that fires when attempts fail to load a corpus into the brain. Next is the initialize method which takes a required keyword parameter inputs_path argument and stores it as an instance variable. After that, a new TemporaryDictionary object is created using MarkyMarkov and stored as a separate instance variable before loading the corpus into this object. Immediately after the constructor is a generate_n_words method that delegates to MarkyMarkov. The intent here is to make a request of Lita: "give me a string of corpus-inspired gibberish of a certain length."

You need to set up some perfunctory unit testing of this public interface by spinning up a new brain, feeding it an abbreviated test corpus, and verifying that the brain faithfully generates tripe on demand:

```
lita-markov-blabber/spec/lita/markov_brain_spec.rb
require 'spec_helper'

describe Lita::MarkovBrain do
  # connect a sample corpus folder from the ./dict folder
  #   of this repository
  let(:test_inputs_path) { File.join(__dir__, '..', '..', 'dict') }

  describe 'given a short file full of words' do
    # load up a brain using the test corpus supplied above
    subject { Lita::MarkovBrain.new(inputs_path: test_inputs_path) }
```

```ruby
  # confirm basic functionality
  it "can generate n words on demand" do
    n = rand(1..100)
    result = subject.generate_n_words(n)

    expect(result.split.count).to eq(n)
  end

end

end
```

Fill your brain with Melville

The private bits of your MarkovBrain class are a bit more interesting than those visible above the waterline. As you'll see momentarily, the implementation of load_brain! takes the previously supplied input_path, interprets it as a folder on the local file system, and feeds any text files in that folder into the brain as bits of the corpus.

First, let's fill up your Markov brain with some classic literature; Herman Melville's *Moby Dick* will do nicely. You can find a .txt file of the entire book on Project Gutenberg.[1] Download the 2701-0.txt file (the full text of Moby Dick) and place it in a new dict subdirectory: lita-markov-blabber/dict/2701-0.txt. The dict folder is where your brain looks to find input texts.

lita-markov-blabber/lib/lita/markov_brain.rb
```ruby
private

# expose .dictionary and .inputs_path
#   as private getters for this class
attr_reader :dictionary, :inputs_path

# Note the short-circuit behavior if the brain is already loaded.
# Raise the custom exception if no suitable inputs are identified.
def load_brain!
  return unless dictionary.dictionary.empty?
  text_files_path = inputs_path + '/*.txt'

  files = Dir[text_files_path]

  if files.none?
    raise(NoBrainInputsFound,
        "No markov input files found at [#{text_files_path}]")
  end

  Dir[text_files_path].each do |file|
    load_dictionary(file)
  end
end
```

---

1. http://www.gutenberg.org/files/2701/

```ruby
def load_dictionary(path)
  logger.debug "Loading Markov input text at: [#{path}]"
  dictionary.parse_file path
end

# Redefine a local logger variable so we can easier test this class
#   in isolation without having to monkeypatch Lita.logger later.
def logger
  Lita.logger
end
```

There are a few interesting things to note about the brain's private implementation. For instance, attribute readers are needed to pass around the dictionary and inputs_path objects. The load_brain! method short-circuits if the brain isn't empty and uses Ruby's File API to check input_path for any available text files before sending them to load_dictionary. When no text files are available, your custom error type is used. This error message explicitly mentions the path it tried to load so end users can trace problems in their attempts to specify an input path. The load dictionary method wraps a call to MarkyMarkov's brain-training parse file code. This saves users of your Lita Markov brain wrapper from having to know too much about MarkyMarkov's more general purpose API.

Build a Lita handler for the brain

You need to fill out the MarkovBlabber Lita handler you generated earlier. This will capture a new :unhandled_message Lita event type and ask your Markov brain for a response. Note in the code listing that you'll set up a default value for the brain's inputs path and assign it to a Lita configuration option.

lita-markov-blabber/lib/lita/handlers/markov_blabber.rb
```ruby
class MarkovBlabber < Handler

  # e.g. lita-markov-brain/dict/name-of-input-file.txt
  DEFAULT_INPUTS_PATH = File.join __dir__, '..', '..', '..', 'dict'

  # allow end user to set their own input path at runtime
  config :markov_inputs_path, default: DEFAULT_INPUTS_PATH

  # redirect ALL otherwise unexpected chat messages to blabber
  on :unhandled_message, :blabber

  def blabber(payload)
    payload.fetch(:message).reply gibberish
  end

  def gibberish
    n = rand(5..20)
    gibberish = brain.generate_n_words n
  end
```

The gibberish method leverages the generate_n_words functionality you've hoisted up from MarkyMarkov to generate a string of five to twenty words from your input text, in this case *Moby Dick*. The blabber event handler method requests some gibberish and sends it back to the chat channel where the unhandled message originated. The private section of your MarkovBlabber wraps a class instance variable, @@brain, that helps Lita keep the same Markov brain in memory from one minute to the next for efficiency reasons.

lita-markov-blabber/lib/lita/handlers/markov_blabber.rb
```ruby
private

# define as a persistent class instance variable so you're not recreating
#   and reloading the brain on each incoming message.
def brain
  @@brain ||= Lita::MarkovBrain.new(inputs_path: config.markov_inputs_path)
end
```

Test the Markov handler

Testing this handler requires a bit of ceremony to get started, because you need to feed your brain some input text before you can use it.

Create another new dict folder inside ./spec and place a short snippet of your full-sized Melville input. This speeds up your test runs without compromising the spirit of your unit tests.

Note the before do block at the top of the file; this is necessary to inject the desired input path configuration before your test objects are set up.

lita-markov-blabber/spec/lita/handlers/markov_blabber_spec.rb
```ruby
# e.g. lita-markov-blabber/spec/dict/moby-dick-sample.txt
let(:test_inputs_path) { File.join(__dir__, '..', '..', 'dict') }

let(:robot) { Lita::Robot.new(registry) }

# preload a test inputs path to your already started markov blabber module
before do
  robot.config.handlers.markov_blabber.markov_inputs_path = test_inputs_path
end

# manually set up a new lita bot as the system under test
#   since the default behavior can't quite link this together
subject { described_class.new(robot) }
```

Test both public methods for your handler.

lita-markov-blabber/spec/lita/handlers/markov_blabber_spec.rb
```ruby
# test base case of generating N words on demand
describe ':gibberish' do
  it 'generates lots of words' do
    result = subject.gibberish
    word_count = result.split.count
```

```
      expect(word_count > 4).to be_truthy
      expect(word_count < 30).to be_truthy
    end
  end

# confirm variations on "words come in, words go out"
describe 'blabber' do
  it 'answers arbitrary inputs' do
    lyrics = ['welcome to the jungle',
              'take me down to the paradise city',
              "shed a tear cause i'm missing you"]

    lyrics.each do |lyric|
      send_message lyric
      response = replies.last
      word_count = response.split.count

      expect(word_count > 4).to be_truthy
      expect(word_count < 30).to be_truthy
    end
  end
end
```

The test for the gibberish method is straightforward. You need to verify that it generates a few handfuls of whitespace-delimited tokens that you can safely assume are words. As for the blabber test, it runs an end-to-end simulation of the final product by sending in three lines of text, one at a time, and verifying that Lita responds with another handful of words each time.

Now that the Markov chain skill is ready to use, it's time for a test run. Go ahead and interrogate your Melville-trained Lita bot with some *Jabberwocky* quotes and see what you get back:

```
BookBot > 'Twas brillig, and the slithey toves
Lord; though in some very out of others' hearts what's
BookBot > Did gyre and gimble in the wabe
"Captain, I have a chat with the people of the boys, if boys there be aboard.
```

Great, it looks like Lita can hold her own when faced with unexpected or irregular inputs. As a stretch goal, you might want to consider having this skill roll the dice and only respond 5 or 10% of the time, rather than every time it sees an unhandled input. There's also some low-hanging fruit regarding the irregular capitalization and punctuation of these auto-generated responses.

Cleverbot: Use an External AI for Difficult Questions

Your next task is to use Cleverbot to handle more difficult questions. Cleverbot is a public chatbot that's been online since 1997. It's designed to remember and reuse lessons learned from human inputs, so the relevance and humanity of responses will be a bit better than those of your naive Markov chain implementation. While Cleverbot is mostly known as a diverting chat bot on a web page, as you can see in the following image, it can also be accessed through an API, which is perfect for Lita's needs.

But before you can use the API, you need to obtain a key.

Acquire a Cleverbot API key

To hook up your Lita bot to Cleverbot, you need to register for a free Cleverbot API key online.[2] The current Cleverbot page suggests that you'll get thousands of free clever responses before the API starts charging a fee. After you're registered, take note of both your Cleverbot username and its API key. Each of these are strings that you'll feed into Lita as configuration options.

Wire Cleverbot into a Lita handler

Create a new Lita handler as usual:

lita handler cleverbot-demo.

Switch into the newly generated lita-cleverbot-demo folder and add your Cleverbot API client as a dependency in the gemspec file. The cleverbot_io gem is straightforward enough for Lita purposes, so start with that one.

```
spec.add_dependency "cleverbot_io"
```

2.　https://www.cleverbot.com/api/

Cleverbot configuration

Inside your cleverbot_demo handler implementation, you need to require the cleverbot_io gem. Lita configuration values for cleverbot_user and cleverbot_key fall back to host environment variables of the same names in case the bot that's using this handler doesn't have its lita_config.rb fully fleshed out.

For now, rather than set up a second unhandled_message catcher, use a simple route that matches inputs like "Lita cleverbot hello there!"

lita-cleverbot-demo/lib/lita/handlers/cleverbot_demo.rb
```
require 'cleverbot'

module Lita
  module Handlers
    class CleverbotDemo < Handler
      # allow user to set API keys as environment variables
      #   or via lita_config.rb
      config :cleverbot_user, default: ENV.fetch('CLEVERBOT_USER')
      config :cleverbot_key, default: ENV.fetch('CLEVERBOT_KEY')

      # note this route's regex is more open-ended than usual!
      route(/^cleverbot (.+)$/i, :handle_cleverbot)
```

Letting Melville and Cleverbot both respond to every incoming message seems like overkill.

Integrate Cleverbot into your handler

The next step is to connect to the Cleverbot API in your client method and then route Lita messages to and from the client with handle_cleverbot and ask_cleverbot.

lita-cleverbot-demo/lib/lita/handlers/cleverbot_demo.rb
```
# directly forward the latest incoming message to cleverbot and
#   send cleverbot's response to the chat channel
def handle_cleverbot(payload)
  clever_input = payload.matches.last

  payload.reply ask_cleverbot(clever_input)
end

def ask_cleverbot(question)
  client.say question
end

# manage a persistent connection to the Clever API throughout the lifecycle
#   of each request
def client
  @_client ||= Cleverbot.new(config.cleverbot_user, config.cleverbot_key)
end
```

You're ready to perform some perfunctory tests against your Cleverbot handler.

Test your Cleverbot handler

You need to verify that Lita is routing messages like "Lita cleverbot hello" and ignoring messages that don't quite match. You also want to make sure that when you feed Lita a question for Cleverbot, you get a response with at least one word.

lita-cleverbot-demo/spec/lita/handlers/cleverbot_demo_spec.rb
```ruby
describe Lita::Handlers::CleverbotDemo, lita_handler: true do
  # verify basic chat routes are matched
  it { is_expected.to route('Lita cleverbot hello') }
  it { is_expected.to_not route('Lita clever hello') }

  # sanity check on basic "questions are answered" function
  describe 'ask cleverbot a question' do
    context 'given an english input' do
      let(:question) { 'hi cleverbot' }
      let(:result) { subject.ask_cleverbot question }

      it 'fetches a response with more than one word' do
        word_count = result.split.count

        expect(word_count).to be > 1
        expect(result).to match(/\w+/)
      end
    end
  end

  # confirm end to end functionality - arbitrary text gets a response
  describe 'lita integration test' do
    it 'answers questions with cleverbot' do
      send_message 'Lita cleverbot hello cleverbot'

      expect(replies.last).to match(/\w+/)
    end
  end
end
```

It's worth noting that in a production scenario, you may want to dig into these objects with stubs and mocks to verify that the appropriate question is sent to the appropriate Cleverbot API client. But for now, this is sufficient.

With your implementation and tests wrapped up, you're ready to take Cleverbot for a spin. Be sure to provide your Cleverbot credentials as environment variables when you launch lita.

```
>>> env CLEVERBOT_USER="username_redacted" \
        CLEVERBOT_KEY="api_key_redacted" bundle exec lita
Type "exit" or "quit" to end the session.
BookBot > bookbot cleverbot good morning
How are you doing?
BookBot > bookbot cleverbot fine thank you
```

```
So what are you doing?
BookBot > bookbot cleverbot I am building chatbots and drinking coffee.
What music?
BookBot > bookbot cleverbot I am listening to some electronic
  dance stuff, you?
Same.
```

You can see that Cleverbot's responses are slightly more relevant and modern sounding than those of your Melville brain. It's up to you to decide whether you'd like this Cleverbot integration to respond only on command or to loiter around grabbing unhandled Lita inputs like your MarkovBlabber.

Wrap-up

In this chapter, you developed some helpful new chatbot skills, and as a result, your Lita bots can now catch and handle inputs that aren't grabbed by your single-purpose skills.

You also set up a new Ruby class outside of a handler. For that, you worked through some file path and test setup subtleties, which you can use and refer back to when you're ready to build more complex Lita skills.

Finally, you integrated Lita with another external service, Cleverbot, which will be particularly entertaining to your chat room's users.

Next, you move onto ChatOps and give Lita some concierge skills, starting with the ability to send text messages and emails.

Challenges

- Melville is charming, but he might not provide the voice you want for your Lita bot. Create your own Markov input text files using lyrics from your favorite band[3] or scripts from your favorite movies.[4]

- Rather than pre-load your Markov bot skill with an existing corpus of speech, try adding new Lita chat routes to enable your users to train the bot from your chat room. You could even instruct Lita to "overhear" and train based on all incoming text, if you set command: false in your training route.

- Cleverbot's API responses include advanced information that the cleverbot_io gem (selected for this chapter) omits. Consider building your own Cleverbot client to give yourself greater customizability.

---

3. https://www.lyrics.com/
4. https://www.imsdb.com/

## CHAPTER 11

Send Messages with SMS and Email

As a bot owner or career software developer, you can expect to send and receive plenty of emails, text messages, and other alerts. Because chat is a conversational medium, sending and receiving messages with Lita is a natural fit.

In this chapter, you'll build two similar message-sending Lita skills as you learn how to push messages beyond the confines of your bot and out into the real world. By the end of this chapter, you'll have a firm grasp on two of the most common communication media for automation: emails and SMS messages.

Use Twilio to Send Text Messages

Twilio is a service that provides powerful API access to send and receive phone calls and text messages. The possibilities for group calls and texts, scripted answering services, and voicemail recording are quite broad. Even non-developers are likely to encounter Twilio-based products, though they might not realize it.

Any sort of phone automation you can imagine is plausible with Twilio—from robocalling to answering to recording to re-routing to messaging; it's all in the API. In this section, you get your feet wet by sending text messages through the service. The first step is signing up for a new account at twilio.com.

Twilio signup is straightforward—you need an email address and a credit card. Don't worry about a charge yet; Twilio includes promotional credits for first-time users. The promotional credits cover the small monthly fee for renting the phone number that sends your messages, as well as a per-message fee for sending text messages.

Once you're registered, you need to claim a local phone number that Twilio can use for sending outbound messages. The first screenshot on page 122 shows the confirmation dialog for selecting a Memphis-area number.

Send a text message with the Twilio API

Armed with your first Twilio outbound phone number, you can move right into sending your first Twilio-powered text message. Like most of the APIs used in this book, the core is a single HTTP transaction. Twilio's docs are particularly good at guiding you to this first successful transaction, including a cURL command tailored to send a message with your newly registered account. Copy and paste the command from your browser—it'll look like the following screenshot—and run it in your terminal.

When you execute the command, you see a JSON response detailing the successful delivery. You should also receive the sample text message at the destination number you supplied.

Here's a sample Twilio response from a successful SMS delivery.

```
# n.b. api keys and message IDs truncated to fit the page
{
  "sid": "SM4625ac9f0cda43c7a36c92e9212c06ef",
  "date_created": "Sun, 19 Nov 2017 20:42:59 +0000",
```

```
"date_updated": "Sun, 19 Nov 2017 20:42:59 +0000", "date_sent": null,
"account_sid": "user_id_redacted", "to": "+12135551234",
"from": "+19014727826", "messaging_service_sid": null,
"body": "Sent from your Twilio trial account - Hello reader!",
  "status": "queued",
"num_segments": "1", "num_media": "0", "direction": "outbound-api",
"api_version": "2010-04-01", "price": null, "price_unit": "USD",
  "error_code": null,
"error_message": null,
"uri": "/2010-04-01/Accounts/user_id_redacted/Messages/SMxxx.json",
"subresource_uris":
  {
    "media": "/2010-04-01/Accounts/id_redacted/Messages/SMxxx/Media.json"
  }
}
```

Your next task is to create a new Lita handler skill that leverages Twilio's Ruby gem to send text messages on demand.

Configure a Twilio handler for Lita

As with every user-facing Lita skill, you need to generate a new handler that listens for a specific pattern of input and responds with some relevant Ruby automation. In this case, your input looks like "send a text message," and the automation shuffles the text message off to Twilio's API.

Start by creating a new Lita handler skill:

```
$ lita handler twilio-texter
```

Switch into the newly created lita-twilio-texter folder and complete the empty parts of your gemspec file. Be sure to add the dependency on twilio-ruby to your own gemspec as demonstrated on line 11.

```
Line 1  # lita-twilio-texter.gemspec

-       Gem::Specification.new do |spec|
-         spec.name          = "lita-twilio-texter"
5
-         # ... snipped boilerplate ...

-         spec.add_runtime_dependency "lita", ">= 4.7"

10        # don't forget this part!
-         spec.add_runtime_dependency 'twilio-ruby', '~> 5.5'

-         # ... snipped more boilerplate ...
-       end
```

Build and test the Twilio handler

The Twilio gem's documentation[1] walks you through the basics of setting up a Twilio connection and sending a message from Ruby. Connecting to Twilio requires an account SID and an auth token. You can think of these as a username and password. These credentials are available from the Twilio web UI, and you'll see them as HTTP parameters in the cURL command you just sent to test your first message.

Connect to Twilio from Ruby

Set up the Twilio connection inside the lita-twilio-texter handler file:

```
# lib/lita/handlers/twilio_texter.rb

config :twilio_sid,   default: ENV['TWILIO_ACCOUNT_SID']
config :twilio_token, default: ENV['TWILIO_AUTH_TOKEN']

def client
  @_client ||= Twilio::REST::Client.new(
    config.twilio_sid,
    config.twilio_token
  )
end
```

With this code, you:

- Provide a way for the calling code (your Lita bot) to inject Twilio credentials with either Lita config variables or regular environment variables.

- Create a RESTful Twilio connection object with the :client method.

- Store a connection as a reusable instance variable.

- Return the connection for in-line use.

The code that calls the :client method eventually reads something like this:

```
client.send_text_message(from: me, to: you, body: user_supplied_message).
```

Next, you need a simple test to verify that the returned client object looks correct.

```
# spec/lita/handlers/twilio_texter_spec.rb

describe ':client' do
  it 'should return a logged-in Twilio client' do
    clt = subject.client
    expect(clt.account_sid.empty?).to be_falsey
    expect(clt.auth_token.empty?).to be_falsey
  end
end
```

---

1.   https://github.com/twilio/twilio-ruby

This test verifies that the returned object has a non-blank login and password and implicitly affirms that calls to the :client don't throw an exception. If everything passes, you can be confident that your Twilio client is configured correctly and available for the SMS sending code you're about to write.

Use a Ruby Connection to Send a Twilio SMS

With a properly configured Twilio client object, you're ready to send your first Twilio SMS from within Ruby. Copy the following example code to provide a :send_twilio_sms call that accepts a destination phone number and a message body.

```
# lib/lita/handlers/twilio_texter.rb

def send_twilio_sms(to:, body:)
  response = client.api.account.messages.create(
    from: send_from_number,
    to: to,
    body: body
  )
end

def send_from_number
  client.incoming_phone_numbers.page.first.phone_number
end
```

Note the inclusion of the :send_from_number helper method. This code is necessary because Twilio's API supports high-volume users with a pool of phone numbers available to them. For your bot, however, you only need one, so the code lazily picks the first available number. In a more sophisticated application, you might choose numbers based on proximity to the end user or other business rules.

You can use the following tests to verify that things are working as intended. Note, however, that these tests—as written—are dependent on hard-coded phone numbers. In production, and for more robust tests, you may want to inject known good numbers at runtime or use an HTTP testing library like WebMock.[2]

```
# spec/lita/handlers/twilio_texter_spec.rb

# your phone number goes here
#   twilio insists you text 'verified' numbers during trial
describe ':send_twilio_sms' do
  it 'should work' do
    response = subject.send_twilio_sms(
      to: '+12135551234',
      body: 'hi from lita test')
```

---

2.   https://github.com/bblimke/webmock

```
    expect(response.error_code).to eq(0)
    expect(response.status).to eq("queued")
  end
end

# also dependent on your trial number's area code
describe ':send_from_number' do
  it 'should return my trial number' do
    number = subject.send_from_number
    expect(number.start_with?('+1213')).to be_truthy
  end
end
```

By verifying that the returned objects are at least behaving like properly instrumented Twilio API objects, you can be somewhat sure your bot's ready to go.

Enable Lita users to send SMS messages using a Twilio wrapper

Your Ruby handler code now has an entry point for your Lita skill, and your users' Lita invocation will look like this:

Lita text 12135551234 hi mom

The following code is similar to other Lita handlers from earlier chapters: this time, it includes a route matcher and a handler method—:send_text—to receive the matches.

```
Line 1  # lib/lita/handlers/twilio_texter.rb

        route /^text\s+(\d+)\s+(.+)$/i,
          :send_text,
     5    command: true,
          help: { 'text 12135551234 hi mom' =>
            'texts "hi mom" to a fake number in California' }

        def send_text(message)
    10      _, to, body = message.match_data.to_a
          results = send_twilio_sms(to: to, body: body)

          message.reply "Sent message to #{to}"
        end
```

Note that on line 3, the matcher expression triggers on the leading word "text," captures the number immediately following, and then captures the remainder of the input as the body of the text message; and on line 10, is a bit of Ruby destructuring (teasing the contents of a data structure apart into multiple variables) to parse the needed parts out of the regex match for safekeeping. The underscore (_) means you're purposefully discarding the first element in the match array.

To verify that things are working, you need some tests.

```ruby
# spec/lita/handlers/twilio_texter_spec.rb
describe ':text' do
  it { is_expected.to route("Lita text 12134441234 hi mom") }
  it { is_expected.to_not route("Lita text hi mom") }

  it 'sends texts' do
    send_message 'Lita text 12135551234 hey daniel'
    expect(replies.last).to eq('Sent message to 12135551234')
  end
end
```

This test asserts that the Lita text [number] [message] handler catches properly formed inputs. It also asserts that Lita's reply to a valid request includes the expected response.

Use SMTP to Send an Email

Sending an email with Lita looks a lot like sending a text message. However, instead of Twilio, you'll use Ruby's built-in mail gem to send messages through an SMTP server; A personal Gmail account using the Google SMTP servers will suffice.

Using Gmail with Your Bot

Gmail is an easy-to-implement example. However, it's not necessarily the most secure nor the highest-throughput solution. If you plan to use Gmail, take steps to protect your private email before you take this skill live. One option is to create a separate Gmail account. Another option is to use a more production-oriented email service like Postmark or Sendgrid.

Configure an SMTP handler for Lita

If you want your Lita users to send emails from their chat rooms, you need to create another Lita handler skill. The following command creates an empty mail Lita skill named smtp-mailer:

```
$ lita handler smtp-mailer
```

You don't need to add extra dependencies to the lita-smtp-mailer.gemspec file, because everything this chapter requires is already in the Ruby standard library. You do, however, need to update the gemspec to use your name, contact info, and license information. If you don't have a preference for license type, opt for the MIT license.

Joe asks:
What is an MIT license?

The MIT software license is a particularly permissive open-source license popular with the authors of software libraries. Library authors might choose it because it ensures that they receive credit for their work while placing minimal restrictions on the users of the MIT licensed software. If you're hoping for a broad install base for your library, choose a permissive license like MIT. If you're hoping to make money directly off of your code or prevent others from reselling it, choose a more restrictive license.

Send your first email from Lita

In this section you'll build a Lita emailer skill using the following steps:

- Find your connection credentials.
- Build the connection info into Lita as config variables.
- Write a Ruby method to send an email to a recipient.
- Build a Lita route and handler to leverage your "send an email" method.

Find your connection credentials

For this example, you can use a Gmail account. They're free and offer accessible SMTP services.

```
Server: smtp.gmail.com
Port: 587 (TLS required)
Username: Your email account name
Password: Your email password
```

To allow a Gmail account to send mail by a generic SMTP client, follow the instructions on the "Let Less Secure Apps Use Your Account" page.[3] Once done, you can find the server address and port information on Google's help site.[4] You will inject the connection info into your Lita skill as config variables.

```ruby
# lib/lita/handlers/smtp_mailer.rb

config :smtp_server, default: 'smtp.gmail.com'
config :smtp_password, default: ENV['SMTP_PASSWORD']
config :smtp_username, default: ENV['SMTP_USERNAME']
config :smtp_from_address, default: nil
config :smtp_auth, default: 'plain'
config :smtp_port, default: 587
config :smtp_enable_tls_auto, default: true
```

---

3. https://support.google.com/accounts/answer/6010255?hl=en
4. https://support.google.com/a/answer/176600?hl=en

Note that the defaults are all Gmail specific, but consumers of your Lita skill are still able to inject settings appropriate to their chosen mail service.

Initialize the mail library defaults

Now that you've gathered your SMTP credentials and injected them into your Ruby runtime as config variables, you're ready to set up the mail library.

```ruby
# lib/lita/handlers/smtp_mailer.rb

require 'mail'

def configure_smtp!
  options = { :address             => config.smtp_server,
              :port                => config.smtp_port,
              :user_name           => config.smtp_username,
              :password            => config.smtp_password,
              :authentication      => config.smtp_auth,
              :enable_starttls_auto => config.smtp_enable_tls_auto }

  Mail.defaults do
    delivery_method :smtp, options
  end
end
```

Here, you add the mail gem at the top of the file and set up a method to configure the sending options. The :configure_smtp method fires before the method that actually sends the mail. The Mail.defaults method call gathers the login, password, SMTP server location, and security requirements.

Before moving on, you need to implement some proper tests.

```ruby
# spec/lita/handlers/smtp_mailer_spec.rb

describe ':configure_smtp!' do
  before { subject.configure_smtp! }
  let(:settings) { Mail.delivery_method.settings }

  it 'should set a password' do
    expect(settings.fetch(:password)).to_not be_nil
  end

  it 'should set a port' do
    expect(settings.fetch(:port)).to eq(587)
  end
end
```

With this test, you assert that your configuration includes some expected non-nil values and incidentally, proves that the call to configure SMTP did not throw an exception.

Send an email with Ruby

Your Lita-managed emails are simple by design: a single recipient and a plain-text payload. The following method illustrates a "send this email to that address" method. It starts by invoking the :configure_smtp method. Usually, you'd expect to see that sort of thing in the class initializer method, but Lita's initializers aren't designed to be easily serviceable.

```ruby
# lib/lita/handlers/smtp_mailer.rb
def deliver_email(to_address:, message_body:,
                  from_address: config.smtp_from_address)
  configure_smtp!

  result = Mail.deliver do
    to to_address
    from from_address
    subject "[Lita bot] #{message_body.first(64)}"
    body message_body
  end
end
```

The actual mail delivery is handled with a call to Mail.deliver that takes a block of configuration calls inside it: to, from, subject, and body. The subject is a chopped-down version of the one-line email body. Note that the from address defaults to be the same as the to address; this helps simplify things in user testing and still allows the flexibility of specifying a from address when you're ready to send this to production.

The testing for the "deliver email via smtp" method covers a few bases:

- The method call doesn't throw an exception.
- The mailer is configured to throw exceptions on delivery.
- The mailer method received the expected recipient email address.

One nice thing about writing unit tests in an object-oriented situation is that in a command testing situation like this, all you need to test is whether the expected external method was invoked with the expected parameters. The actual behavior of the mail gem and its SMTP code is outside the scope of your Lita tests; knowing that you made the right call is sufficient.

```ruby
# spec/lita/handlers/smtp_mailer_spec.rb
describe ':deliver_email smtp method' do
  it 'succeeds' do
    recipient = 'dpritchett@gmail.com'
    result = subject.deliver_email(
      to_address: recipient, message_body: 'hello daniel')
```

```
    expect(result.to_addrs.include?(recipient)).to be_truthy
    expect(result.error_status).to be_nil
  end

  it 'is configured to raise exceptions on delivery failure' do
    result = subject.deliver_email(
      to_address: 'dpritchett+test_lita@gmail.com',
      message_body: 'hello from lita test')

    expect(result.raise_delivery_errors).to be_truthy
  end
end
```

Route commands to your SMTP method

Just like with the Twilio example, you need to build a modest Lita route and
handler method to use your new one-shot email sender method. The following
example contains the remaining implementation code for the SMTP mailer
method: a route that catches an intent to deliver emails, and a handler method
that teases the email address and message body out of chat submissions and
shuttles them off to your mail sender.

```
# lib/lita/handlers/smtp_mailer.rb

# non-whitespace-chars@non-whitespace-chars
SIMPLE_EMAIL_REGEX = /\S+@\S+/

route /^email\s+(#{SIMPLE_EMAIL_REGEX})\s+(.+)$/i,
  :send_email,
  command: true,
  help: {
    'email address@domain.com message body goes here' => 'Sends an email' }

def send_email(response)
  to_address, message_body = response.matches.last
  result = deliver_email to_address: to_address, message_body: message_body
  response.reply "Sent email to [#{to_address}]."
end
```

The most interesting part is the regular expression in the route call. While it's
impossible to craft the perfect regex to capture every email address—and
nothing else—this one does well enough for modest usage.

You need to confirm with tests that Lita triggers as expected.

```
# spec/lita/handlers/smtp_mailer_spec.rb

describe ':send_email' do
  it { is_expected.to route(
    "Lita email dpritchett@gmail.com Hi daniel from lita tests") }
  it { is_expected.to route("Lita email dpritchett@gmail.com hello") }
  it { is_expected.to route("Lita email daniel@localhost hello") }
```

```
it { is_expected.to_not route("Lita email daniel") }
it { is_expected.to_not route("Lita email dpritchett@gmail.com") }

it 'emails numbers' do
  send_message 'Lita email dpritchett@gmail.com Hi daniel from lita tests'
  expect(replies.last.include?('dpritchett@gmail.com')).to be_truthy
end
end
```

This test confirms that three different properly formed commands are all caught by Lita and that nothing will happen if an end user leaves out the email address or the message body. There's also an end-to-end integration test that confirms Lita properly acknowledges that email commands have been handled.

That's it—that's all the code you need. Add both your mail sender (and your SMS sender) to your local Lita bot and enjoy sending messages on demand from chat.

Wrap-up

In this chapter, you had more practice integrating with third-party HTTP APIs. You also integrated a messaging protocol that built on the Ruby standard library rather than a private company's HTTP API.

Up next is a chapter on the care and feeding of a Lita bot. You'll teach Lita to execute local system commands for you and to inspect local files to figure out which version of a given Ruby gem is installed.

Later, in Serve Up a "Flash Briefing" Newsfeed for Echo Devices, on page 146, you'll learn how to instrument Lita skills to enable companion skills to use their code. It's easy to imagine a future skill that also sends an email as part of a larger task.

Challenges

- Now that your Lita users can craft entire messages to anyone they want from their chat room, see whether you can provide them with some pre-configured message options. Maybe you want them to be able to page you or another chat admin? Add a new "lita page admin" route that sends a canned SMS to the folks in charge of your chat room.

- Software system operators commonly receive email reports informing them of exceptional behaviors in their systems. Try setting up a Lita "overheard" skill (again, command: false) to email you whenever a key phrase is uttered in Lita's chat room.

- Build out Lita's observational capabilities: leverage some of the skills you built in the Task Scheduler chapter to automate sending of some emails every day at noon. Maybe you can even track chatroom statistics in Redis and then email yourself the stats every 24 hours.

## CHAPTER 12

ChatOps Techniques for Managing Software Systems

This chapter introduces some Lita-based "ChatOps" techniques. You'll use your Lita bot to help manage, monitor, and control your deployed software systems. ChatOps is a powerful, enjoyable method of sharing the care and feeding of real-world production software. Some of the highlights:

- Teams can have a shared record of software operation actions taken when they're performed in a shared chat room.

- Chat as a user interface provides for a bit of camaraderie and fun in the day-to-day operations of software systems.

- Watching other folks' ChatOps commands in your shared channel allows for low-friction learning. When you see a teammate doing real work with a Lita bot, you pick up on some techniques and practices just by watching.

- Non-engineers can still peek in on your ChatOps rooms to get a feel for the current tempo of releases, changes, and issues of your production systems.

- Lita's ChatOps skills can be mixed in with other bots and monitoring platforms in a shared stream where appropriate.

You'll first teach Lita how to determine which version of a Git repository or a Ruby gem is running. Knowing which version of an application is currently deployed is tremendously useful for software operators. It helps you debug anomalous behavior, keep track of when and whether deployments happened, and make sure you're testing against the version you think you're testing.

This type of problem comes up frequently when you have lots of services and teammates working together to manage them.

Create a Mini-skill to Check Installed Version

For this section, let's assume that your Lita bot is managed by Git and that it has access to a local Git client through your shell. With your bot being part of a locally managed Git repository, you can quickly look up several useful bits of information about your bot:

- What is the git commit hash for the current commit?
- What is the origin URL of this local Git repository?
- What is the installed version of this Lita skill's gem?

The following demo session asks a Lita bot named "Bookbot" which version of its codebase is running. Behind the scenes, Lita executes a few shell commands to find out which git commit is currently active and which version of a specific gem is installed. Lita then presents those data points in a chat-friendly format.

lita-version-check/examples/001-demo.session
```
> bundle exec lita
Type "exit" or "quit" to end the session.
BookBot > bookbot version check
My git revision is [fc648e78f54a74ca92a82d0ff77a9151fcf8e373].
My repository URL is [git@github.com:dpritchett/ruby-bookbot.git].
<<<>>>
Brought to you by [lita-version-check 0.1.0].
```

Now it's your turn to create a new Lita handler skill to demonstrate these basic Git interactions.

Run a lita handler version-check command to generate a new Lita skill in its own folder. Inside that folder, you'll find an auto-generated lita-version-check/lib/lita/handlers/version_check.rb file ready for customization.

You'll begin by requiring the open3 module from Ruby's standard library. This one is useful for wrapping calls to operating system commands in a repeatable way.

Next, you'll make a Lita route call that only answers to "version check."

Because the core activity of this skill is going to invoke operating system commands and print their output, you need an :exec_cmd method for executing arbitrary commands. The exec_cmd method doesn't add much on top of Ruby's built-in command execution options, but for the sake of instruction, this chapter gives you a hands-on look at :capture2e. You may want to research other Ruby command invocation idioms. Here's what you'll end up with:

lita-version-check/lib/lita/handlers/version_check.rb

```ruby
require 'open3'

module Lita
  module Handlers
    class VersionCheck < Handler
      # Simple route that responds to `lita version check` and nothing else.
      route(/^version check$/i, :check_version, command: true)

      # Executes a shell command on the host operating system and returns
      #   a combined STDOUT + STDERR string.
      #
      # WARNING: Don't let end users pass arbitrary text to this method!
      #   Also don't run Lita as a privileged user if you can help it.
      def exec_cmd(cmd)
        result, _ = Open3.capture2e(cmd)
        result
      end
```

Your "version check" route passes its input to a new method named :check_version. You'll implement this one as a multiline string that packages up the results of three targeted methods: :git_sha, :git_repository_url, and :gemspec_version:

lita-version-check/lib/lita/handlers/version_check.rb

```ruby
# Builds a string demonstrating the three version checking methods
#   constructed in this chapter: git sha, git repo URL, and gem version.
#
def check_version(message)
  message.reply [
    "My git revision is [#{git_sha}].",
    "My repository URL is [#{git_repository_url}].",
    '<<<>>>',
    "Brought to you by [#{gemspec_version}]."
  ].join("\n")
end
```

Your report requires three bits of information, each of which can be dug up with a short shell command. Lita digs them out one by one and reformats them for the end user's reading. First the bot answers the question, "What's the latest git commit in the active branch?" This is handled in the :git_sha method, a wrapper for git rev-parse HEAD:

lita-version-check/lib/lita/handlers/version_check.rb

```ruby
# Fetch the SHA representing the current git commit in this repository:
#   e.g. fc648e78f54a74ca92a82d0ff77a9151fcf8e373
def git_sha
  exec_cmd("git rev-parse HEAD").strip
end
```

Your next shell one-liner is :gemspec_version, which executes a bundle list command to retrieve a list of the active Ruby gems in the current folder. It then filters the list to only the ones named lita-version-check. The results are slimmed down to the point that you get nothing but the gem version number. For example, the bundle list output for version 0.1.0 initially looks like this:

```
* lita-version-check (0.1.0)
```

The :gemspec_version method strips that verbose gem version description down to a bare 0.1.0 version number.

lita-version-check/lib/lita/handlers/version_check.rb
```
# Asks the bundle command which version of lita-version-check you're
#    running.
#
#    e.g. lita-version-check 0.1.0
#
def gemspec_version
  # - list all installed gems in this context and filter for the one named
  #    version check,
  # - strip out all characters other than alphanumerics and . - and space.
  # - trim leading and trailing whitespace
  # - split on whitespace
  # - join the split tokens back together with a uniform single space
  exec_cmd("bundle list | grep lita-version-check")
    .gsub(/[^A-Za-z0-9\.\- ]/i, '')
    .strip
    .split
    .join(' ')
end
```

The next one-liner is :git_repository_url. It queries the git command for the URL of the open repository's remote origin—in other words, the destination your regular git push commands push to.

lita-version-check/lib/lita/handlers/version_check.rb
```
# Fetch the short-form repository URL of this git repo e.g.
#    git@github.com:dpritchett/ruby-bookbot.git
def git_repository_url
  exec_cmd("git config --get remote.origin.url").strip
end
```

Finally, add an :echo method that provides a basic test interface to confirm that your command executor works as intended. You'll pass in a quote from Master Obi-Wan, and the echo command should spit it right back out.

lita-version-check/lib/lita/handlers/version_check.rb
```
# Simple echo method that exists to give us a simple test for confirming
#    that the command executor works as expected.
def echo_test(message="hi")
  exec_cmd "echo #{message}"
end
```

That concludes the Lita version check skill's base implementation. Now it's time to write some unit tests.

Test the Command Executor

Your version_check_spec.rb file was autogenerated when you created this handler skill. Start it off by adding a test for the :echo_test method that confirms whether or not your command executor works as intended:

lita-version-check/spec/lita/handlers/version_check_spec.rb

```
# Minimal test to confirm that executing commands appears to be
#   happening without throwing an exception.
it "Should successfully execute and echo command and return the input" do
  greeting = "Hello there!"
  result = subject.echo_test(greeting)
  expect(result.strip).to eq(greeting)
end
```

Now that you know your command executor works, you can add some quick unit tests to confirm that your three lookup methods do what they need to do:

lita-version-check/spec/lita/handlers/version_check_spec.rb

```
describe "lookup commands" do
  it "finds a git sha" do
    result = subject.git_sha
    expect(result.strip).to eq(`git rev-parse HEAD`.strip)
  end

  it "finds a gem version from the bundle list command" do
    result = subject.gemspec_version
    expect(result.include? 'lita-version-check').to be_truthy
  end

  it "finds a git repo URL" do
    result = subject.git_repository_url
    # repo url subject to change but that's where the code for this
    #   book is publicly posted.
    expect(result).to match(/git@github.com/)
  end
end
```

That's it for your Lita version checker. Next, a "Ship it!" command that shows how to call on-disk Makefiles and execute a deployment command.

Ask Lita to Ship a New Software Release

This next Lita ChatOps skill demonstrates a basic deployment process: The Lita admin configures a Lita skill to know the location of a specific Makefile and the named deploy task that kicks off a system deploy. In the simplest case, that is make deploy, which is equivalent to make --directory . deploy:

```
lita-makefile-executor/examples/001-demo.session
lita-makefile-executor> lita
lita Type "exit" or "quit" to end the session.
Lita > lita shipit!
make: Entering directory '/media/windows/Users/dpritchett/Documents
  /dpchat/Book/code/lita-makefile-executor/examples'
The time is Sun Jan 13 20:19:48 CST 2019
I'm deploying now wow!
make: Leaving directory '/media/windows/Users/dpritchett/Documents
  /dpchat/Book/code/lita-makefile-executor/examples'
```

What Lita did in this demo is what you're about to implement:

- Hear a "lita shipit!" command.

- Open a Makefile located at a specific location provided as a Lita config variable.

- Execute a single make task from the specified Makefile. The task name (deploy by default) is stored in a second Lita config variable.

Here's the Makefile that executed the example deploy in the previous demo. You can see that it's a simple shell script, but the larger point here is that Lita can kick off more complex shell operations with the same techniques.

```
lita-makefile-executor/examples/Makefile
NOW = $(shell date)
deploy:
        @printf "The time is $(NOW)\n"
        @printf "I'm deploying now wow!\n"
```

While this particular Makefile is purposefully simple, teams around the world can and do use make for deploying their professional production applications. At the end of the chapter are some challenges to grow these techniques into more flexible, real-world solutions.

Create a new handler skill by executing lita handler makefile_executor at the command line. After the new skill is generated, start filling in the makefile_executor.rb with the two config entries:

```
lita-makefile-executor/lib/lita/handlers/makefile_executor.rb
module Lita
  module Handlers
    class MakefileExecutor < Handler
      config :shipit_command, default: 'deploy'
      config :shipit_makefile_path, default: './examples'
```

Now that you have a shipit_command and a shipit_makefile_path, you're ready to build out your new skill's chat route and handler. Match on "ship it" or "shipit" using the pipe-inside-a-parentheses regex form:

lita-makefile-executor/lib/lita/handlers/makefile_executor.rb

```ruby
route /^(shipit|ship it)/i, :shipit_handler, command: true

def shipit_handler(message)
  appname = message.matches.last
  result = ship_app
  message.reply result
end
```

Your "shipit" command captured from the previous snippet calls out to a new :ship_app method, which you still need to create. It's a call to make --directory followed by the contents of your two configuration variables.

lita-makefile-executor/lib/lita/handlers/makefile_executor.rb

```ruby
# Passes a Makefile path and task name to make.
#
# Separates the file and the command in an attempt to limit the
#   blast radius of potential malicious input. Note: you'll
#   probably want to further sanitize this before running it in
#   production or giving it access to login secrets.
#
def ship_app
  `make --directory #{config.shipit_makefile_path} #{config.shipit_command}`
end
```

That's the entirety of the lita shipit! command. It wouldn't be complete without some unit tests, so open the makefile_executor_spec.rb file and type up a few:

lita-makefile-executor/spec/lita/handlers/makefile_executor_spec.rb

```ruby
require "spec_helper"

describe Lita::Handlers::MakefileExecutor, lita_handler: true do
  let(:result) { subject.ship_app }

  # Simple test to confirm that this command executes the deploy
  #   command found in ./examples/Makefile
  it "executes a make command" do
    expect(result).to include('make')
    expect(result).to include('Entering directory')
    expect(result).to include('deploying now wow')
  end

  # End to end test from "lita hears this" to
  #   "lita responds with that"
  it "responds to lita shipit!" do
    send_command("shipit!")
    expect(replies.last).to include('deploying now')
  end
end
```

The most noteworthy part of that test file is that it relies on the default values of the Lita config variables to stay at ./examples and deploy to pass the unit tests: The expected results are what you get when you run that example Makefile.

Your makefile executor skill is complete.

Wrap-up

The ChatOps tasks you built in this chapter give you a solid introduction to what Lita can do as a part of your DevOps process. You know how to see which git version a live chatbot is running. You know how to trigger a deploy from a local Makefile.

In the next chapter, you'll create a pair of skills leveraging an Amazon Echo device to connect Alexa to Lita.

Challenges

There are many things you can bake into a ChatOps setup:

- You can have an external build server call into your Lita bot using a webhook to announce[1] build results. I wrote one of those for this book but never found a spot for it.

- You could have Lita reach out to your source control system (maybe GitHub) and approve or reject a numbered pull request. This is 100% possible with the GitHub API. Check out the octokit gem for a quick start.

- You can reach out to Docker Hub and tag a specific docker build as production. A separate system can poll your Docker image repository for changes in tags and auto-deploy anything that shows up under that production tag.

- You can use CircleCI's super flexible workflows to do all of the above. CircleCI workflows (and now GitHub Actions) are a *very* powerful way to run repeatable DevOps tasks in a "serverless" environment.

---

1. https://github.com/dpritchett/lita-travis-announcer

## CHAPTER 13

Amazon Alexa Integrations

Voice assistant technology—like Amazon's Alexa, Apple's Siri, and Google Assistant—bring another side of chatbots to phones, cars, and living rooms. As a dedicated bot builder, you may be happy to know that your steadily growing Lita powers can be applied to power the iconic Alexa voice recognition and response skill, as well as the Alexa flash briefing. (Note: Alexa's interactions are commonly referred to as "skills" for the same reasons this book calls Lita interactions skills.)

The primary Alexa interaction is called a custom skill. These are question-and-answer or command interactions like, "Turn on the lights," and "What is today's weather?" The flash briefing is a plain-text newsfeed that Alexa reads aloud when asked, "What's in the news?"

For this chapter, you're going to build a matched pair of Lita handlers. The first handler provides an Alexa flash briefing at a custom URL hosted by your Lita bot. The second handler takes dictation from an Alexa-enabled device and stores that text as a news item in your flash briefing queue. Armed with these two working proofs of concept, you'll be ready to create a broad variety of Alexa integrations.

Hardware, Simulators, and Alexa Portal Access

Although this chapter is more fun with a physical Alexa-enabled device, like the Echo Dot, you can work through these exercises using a web-based simulator. With Echosim[1] (shown in the screenshot on page 144) and an Amazon account, you can talk to a virtual Echo device that supports most of the standard Alexa functionality.

---

1. http://echosim.io

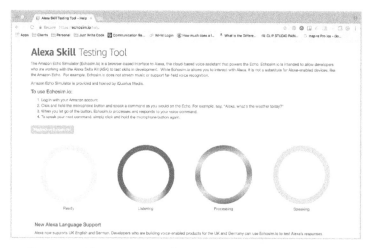

Register for an Alexa Developer Account

Before you can access your soon-to-be-written Lita skills from Alexa devices, you need to create an Amazon developer account. Once you're signed up and logged in, you can create your first Alexa skill on the portal and configure it to point to your bot's URL.

To get started, open https://developer.amazon.com and log in using a free Amazon account. Once logged in, click the Alexa tab, and then click the "Get Started" button located under the "Alexa Skills Kit" section, as shown in the following image.

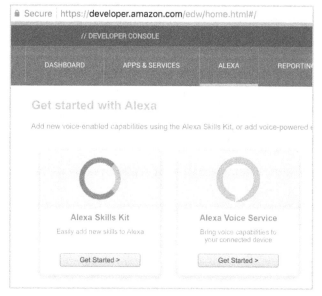

You're ready to start building your first skill.

Create Your First Skill on the Portal

The following screenshot shows the Alexa section of my personal Amazon developer dashboard; you can see the list of skills I've already set up.

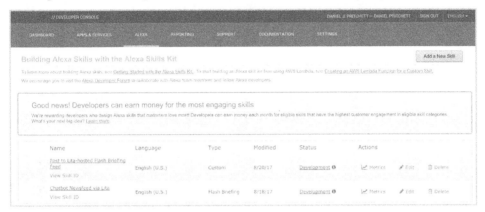

To begin constructing the flash briefing, click "Add a New Skill."

In the "Skill Information" tab, select the "Flash Briefing" option and name the skill "Chatbot Newsfeed via Lita." This is the name users will see in the Alexa app.

News feeds don't have configurable options, so you can skip the "Interaction Model" tab.

Next is the "Configuration" tab (shown in the screenshot on page 146). Your feed needs a name, some descriptive text, and most importantly, the URL where Alexa can find your feed. In this section, you'll enter a preamble, feed metadata, and your feed's production URL.

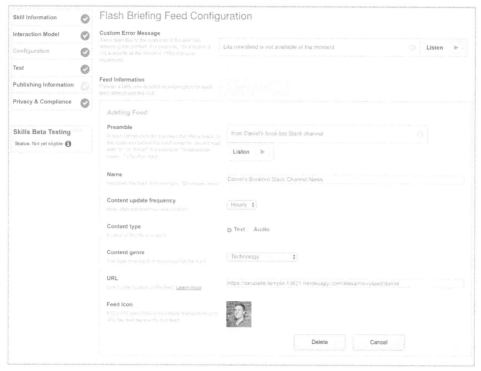

Under the "Test" tab, select "Yes" to show this skill in the Alexa app. This lets you add the briefing to your user account and test the app against your Echo.

On the "Publishing Information" tab, you might want to add an avatar or another useful icon. I do tend to leave this section empty in the proof of concept phase.

Under "Privacy & Compliance," certify that your flash briefing doesn't intend to impinge on any user privacy.

You're now ready to implement your two Alexa skills with Lita, starting with the simpler newsfeed.

Serve Up a "Flash Briefing" Newsfeed for Echo Devices

Alexa's flash briefing is a newsfeed that's similar to a Really Simple Syndication (RSS) feed. When asked, "Alexa, what's in the news?", Alexa's servers send out an HTTP GET request to a preconfigured URL, such as https://your-lita-bot.herokuapp.com/alexa/newsfeed. Your bot returns a JSON-formatted list of news items.

The following is a sample JSON response from a working news feed. Notice the unique identifier (uid) for each post, the timestamp, the embedded URL, and the two text fields. Your Lita skill needs to supply each of those when queried by Alexa.

```
lita-alexa-news-publisher/examples/001_flash_briefing.json
[{
  "uid": "e3d7a7cd-f67d-445b-a1d6-5e5852b63384",
  "updateDate": "2017-08-30T12:33:45Z",
  "titleText": "Lita update",
  "mainText": "hello book",
  "redirectionUrl": "https://github.com/dpritchett/lita-alexa-news-publisher"
}, {
  "uid": "cae6899f-2c72-4a09-bcb7-dc82aded3a41",
  "updateDate": "2017-08-30T12:34:05Z",
  "titleText": "Lita update",
  "mainText": "adding a second post to the news feed",
  "redirectionUrl": "https://github.com/dpritchett/lita-alexa-news-publisher"
}]
```

Your job now is to build a Lita handler that serves up a JSON feed much like the one shown. Once it works, you can set up an Alexa flash briefing skill to poll the feed URL.

Let's go through the finished product, one method at a time, so you can see how it all fits together. You can review the finished code online.[2]

First, you create a new Lita handler skill. You then announce your intentions to accept HTTP GET requests at a particular URL. Since this is a plain GET request, you won't need to specify any specific GET parameters to be handled. The only implicit contract here is that you need to return JSON-formatted text that Amazon's Alexa servers can recognize as a newsfeed. There's a reference spec[3] you can use to design the response payload.

Teach Lita to handle a newsfeed command

The first line in the following snippet is the chatbot-facing interaction that you'll use to fill the newsfeed. Chatroom users type "lita newsfeed hello, world!" A "hello, world" message is then stored in Redis to be retrieved later when Alexa asks (via an HTTP request to your Lita bot) to see the newsfeed. Your :publish_to_newsfeed handler extracts the user's message from the input payload and sends it to Redis with the :save_message call.

---

2. https://github.com/dpritchett/lita-alexa-news-publisher

3. https://developer.amazon.com/public/solutions/alexa/alexa-skills-kit/docs/flash-briefing-skill-api-feed-reference#json-message-examples

lita-alexa-news-publisher/lib/lita/handlers/alexa_news_publisher.rb
```
route(/(newsfeed) (.*)/i, :publish_to_newsfeed)

def publish_to_newsfeed(response)
  msg = response.matches.last.last
  save_message(username: response.user.name, message: msg)

  response.reply("Saved message for Alexa: [#{msg}]")
end
```

Next is the snippet that shows how to accept an HTTP GET request to a specific URL and route it to a particular Lita method.

lita-alexa-news-publisher/lib/lita/handlers/alexa_news_publisher.rb
```
http.get '/alexa/newsfeed/:username', :user_newsfeed
```

Test the newsfeed route

Verifying that a route is established correctly is a one-liner in Lita's RSpec test harness using the route_http helper, shown in the next snippet.

lita-alexa-news-publisher/spec/lita/handlers/alexa_news_publisher_spec.rb
```
describe 'routes' do
  it {
    is_expected.to route_http(:get, '/alexa/newsfeed/a_user_name')
      .to(:user_newsfeed)
  }

  it { is_expected.to route('Lita newsfeed hello, alexa!') }
end
```

Save a new newsfeed message to Redis

After calling a hypothetical :save_message method in the Lita handler method, the next logical thing to do is to implement :save_message. The goals for this are broken out as follows:

- Format a simple hashmap payload containing the message and its relevant metadata.

- Store the hashmap in an array in Lita's in-memory datastore, which is backed by Redis.[4]

- Tend the resulting array of messages to ensure it doesn't carry stale messages longer than necessary.

Look over the :save_message implementation. At the top, you see a new addition to the Lita toolkit: the :on method exposes a named event that allows other Lita handlers to call in to use this code without duplicating any Ruby. Later

---

4.   https://redis.io/

in the chapter, you'll write a Lita skill for taking dictation through Alexa that invokes this :save_alexa_message trigger to save data in the same newsfeed you're building now.

The payload extraction is Ruby, and the keys are named :username, :message, :uuid, and :timestamp. The timestamp is in UTC (an ISO format) for general system hygiene reasons. You may be unfamiliar with the SecureRandom tools from Ruby's standard library—just know that the :uuid method generates a nice long string suitable for use as a non-sequential primary key in many situations.

By calling rpush, you'll write the message to the database. While Lita offers redis.get and redis.set convenience methods for basic use, something more complicated like this array of messages requires the broader Redis API. To reach those methods, you need to call Lita.redis.method_name_here. You can find online the full list of Redis methods exposed by the redis-rb gem[5] that Lita uses under the hood. The rpush method appends the given input to the right-hand side, conceptually the end of a left-to-right list of items. Since the Redis gem automatically serializes as a string any data structure you write to the database, it's best to automatically turn your message payloads into JSON before you send them to the database. You can see the JSON.dump call inside the redis.rpush ensuring that the data is in a format you'll be able to use when you pull it back out.

The rest of :save_message is database housekeeping. There's a call to prune_message_list; you'll implement that later to prevent the array of JSON-formatted messages stored at location STORE_KEY from growing larger than the maximum allowed message count. Because intermittent Redis response errors can occur when implementing this method, wrap it in a try/catch block. This instructs Ruby to "rescue" expected error conditions related to Redis and then retry a few times before giving up. The call to redis.del is useful in development to dump data stored in the target location that doesn't fully conform to the evolving design. If you put in anything other than a Redis array, you'll get a CommandError when you try to rpush to it. That's where the error handling comes in handy.

```
lita-alexa-news-publisher/lib/lita/handlers/alexa_news_publisher.rb
# allow other handlers to send messages through this system
#  usage: robot.trigger(:save_alexa_message,
#          username: 'user', message: 'message')
on :save_alexa_message, :save_message
```

---

5.   http://www.rubydoc.info/github/redis/redis-rb/Redis%3Arpush

```ruby
def save_message(username:, message:)
  payload = {
    username: username,
    message: message,
    uuid: SecureRandom.uuid,  # e.g. 752fc85e-61b1-429f-8a69-cf6e6489c8c1
    timestamp: Time.now.utc.iso8601 # e.g. 2017-08-18T12:59:51Z
  }
  begin
    Lita.redis.rpush(STORE_KEY, JSON.dump(payload))

    prune_message_list!
    payload
  rescue Redis::CommandError
    @retries ||= 0
    @retries += 1

    Lita.redis.del(STORE_KEY)

    if @retries < 5
      retry
    else
      # handle failure
    end
  end
end
```

Test the save message function

You can test the :save_message method with a fairly naive unit test: send it a message and verify that the message is included in Lita's chat reply. This implicitly verifies that the attempt to do so didn't throw any errors, such as the Redis CommandErrors mentioned previously. You can also see an example event trigger test using the route_event test helper method.

lita-alexa-news-publisher/spec/lita/handlers/alexa_news_publisher_spec.rb
```ruby
describe ':save_message' do
  let(:body) { 'hello, alexa!' }
  it 'saves a message and acknowledges' do
    result = subject.save_message(username: 'dpritchett', message: body)

    expect(result.fetch(:message)).to eq body
  end

  it { is_expected.to route_event(:save_alexa_message).to(:save_message) }
end
```

Implement a bounded collection for newsfeed items in Redis

Next is the straightforward method to prune the message list. While you have more messages in the list than you want, pop the oldest message off of the list. Since new messages are pushed to the tail end of the list, you'll discard the oldest message with an lpop off of the front of the list.

```
lita-alexa-news-publisher/lib/lita/handlers/alexa_news_publisher.rb
# only store the latest N messages in redis at a time
def prune_message_list!
  while Lita.redis.llen(STORE_KEY) > MAX_MESSAGE_COUNT do
    Lita.redis.lpop(STORE_KEY)
  end
end
```

Render newsfeed as JSON for the Alexa Web Service

Following is the high-level implementation of the :user_newsfeed method that handles incoming GET requests to return a newsfeed. The basic logic flow of this method is as follows:

- An HTTP request object comes in (a Rack request,[6] specifically).

- The request is parsed.

- You pull the last few messages out of the predetermined Redis register that your other Alexa skill stored them in. You reformat each message into an Alexa-compatible payload.

- You send these formatted responses back to the HTTP client application inside of the Rack::Response object Lita has provided you as a method parameter.

Retrieve stored messages from Redis

The next snippet is the :user_newsfeed method implementation. The first thing to notice is the two constants at the top. STORE_KEY determines the location Lita uses to read and write your constantly shifting list of Alexa-relevant newsfeed items. MAX_MESSAGE_COUNT sets the maximum number of messages you'll accumulate in Redis before you start dropping the oldest messages. On to the method itself, :user_newsfeed takes a request argument and a response argument. These are a Rack::Request supplied by Lita and a matching Rack::Response, also supplied by Lita.

Now you pull all of your previously stored messages out of Redis using the Lita.redis.lrange command. This pulls a specified number of messages from the left, or front, of the array. You will convert the message payloads from JSON strings back to Ruby hashmaps with JSON.parse. Then, you pass

---

6.   http://www.rubydoc.info/gems/rack/Rack/Request

them to the :alexify method to translate the message shape into a format Alexa will accept. Finally, set a JSON header in the Rack response and write the JSON-formatted list of Alexa newsfeed messages back to the waiting HTTP client.

lita-alexa-news-publisher/lib/lita/handlers/alexa_news_publisher.rb
```ruby
STORE_KEY = 'alexa_newsfeed'
MAX_MESSAGE_COUNT = 100

def user_newsfeed(request, response)
  request.env["router.params"][:username]

  messages = Lita.redis.lrange(STORE_KEY, 0, MAX_MESSAGE_COUNT)

  formatted_messages = messages.map do |m|
    alexify JSON.parse(m, symbolize_names: true)
  end

  response.headers["Content-Type"] = "application/json"
  response.write(MultiJson.dump(formatted_messages))
end
```

Format news items as Alexa-compatible JSON

The final method required to implement the flash briefing is :alexify. In this method, you take a hashmap named message, tease out its metadata, and then mush it into an Alexa-friendly hashmap with the required string keys like uid, updateDate, and mainText.

lita-alexa-news-publisher/lib/lita/handlers/alexa_news_publisher.rb
```ruby
def alexify(message)
  host_url = 'https://github.com/dpritchett/lita-alexa-news-publisher'
  main_text = message.fetch(:message)

  {
    "uid": message.fetch(:uuid),
    "updateDate": message.fetch(:timestamp),
    "titleText": "Lita update",
    "mainText": main_text,
    "redirectionUrl": host_url
  }
end
```

To test Alexify, send a message with a predetermined phrase like, "test message," and then verify that the result looks how you expect: a hashmap that allows you to successfully :fetch a mainText attribute.

lita-alexa-news-publisher/spec/lita/handlers/alexa_news_publisher_spec.rb
```ruby
describe ':alexify' do
  let(:message) do
    subject.save_message username: 'daniel', message: 'test message'
  end
```

```
  it 'should return a hash with an alexa-specific shape' do
    result = subject.alexify(message)
    expect(result.fetch(:mainText)).to eq('test message')
  end
end
```

You're done with the flash briefing. You need to select the development-mode skill for your personal Alexa setup using either the Alexa mobile app or the online version at https://alexa.amazon.com/spa/index.html. Under the "Skills" tab, there's a "Your skills" button. Find the Lita skill, click to enable it, and you're ready to go. You can now switch on an Echo device or open Echosim.io and say, "Alexa, what's in the news?" to hear your flash briefing in action.

Your published feed will have its own page on Alexa's index of skills.

In the next section, you'll build a companion Lita skill that takes dictation from Alexa to be added to your flash briefing.

Record Messages with a Companion Alexa Skill

Armed with a working Alexa flash briefing, it's time to add a complementary skill to your Lita bot. Where the first Alexa skill exposed a newsfeed for Alexa to recite, this one allows users to tell Alexa to add new messages to that newsfeed. By building this skill, you learn the rudiments of Alexa's custom skills functionality; this will empower you to build any new Alexa skills you can dream up.

You'll also learn about shared event triggers. With shared event triggers, you can call a Lita skill's exposed functionality from another Lita skill.

Here's a sample dialog of a user interacting with your new skill:

> *User:* "Alexa, tell bot recorder, bowties are cool"
>
> *Alexa:* "Added your message to Lita's flash briefing: 'bowties are cool'"
>
> *User:* "Alexa, what's in the news?"
>
> *Alexa:* "Lita's flash briefing: 'bowties are cool'"

See how Alexa's second response is reading aloud the flash briefing you put together earlier—this demonstrates the interplay between the pair of Alexa-oriented Lita skills. This bot recorder skill doesn't need its own data store on the Lita end; it just passes messages along to the existing flash briefing.

To get this working, you need to learn how Alexa custom skills are configured on Amazon's Alexa skill builder pages. You also need to add an HTTP handler to your Lita bot to correctly handle the requests that Alexa's servers send you after the end user speaks their command.

Your Alexa custom skill's interaction model needs a few pieces to work with the Echo devices:

- A skill name to be used when invoking the skill. You'll use "bot recorder" in this example because Alexa understands it easier than "Lita bot."

- An intent describing the action a user expects from Alexa. In this case, you only have one intent: to record a message. Since there's only one intent, the user doesn't have to say, "record a message." A more complex Alexa skill would require the user to specify which supported intent they're pursuing.

- A slot—anything you want Alexa to capture and send on to your backend. In this case, the slot is the message to be recorded, for example, "bowties are cool." Think of slots like variable capture in a regular expression or an HTML form field.

Before showing the Lita skill that powers the bot recorder backend, let's walk through the Amazon screens.

Configuring your Alexa skill on the developer portal

Just like you did for the previous skill, open the Alexa portal at developer.amazon.com. Click the "Alexa" tab and then click "Alexa Skills Kit." Now, click "Add a New Skill" and select the "Custom" skill type.

You access custom skills by their "Invocation name," as in, "Alexa, ask Lita bot skill to record some news for me." So the first step in configuring your custom skill is to specify that name. Stick with "bot recorder" for now. The "name" field determines what shows up if users search for this skill in the Alexa skills marketplace. You don't need to publish this to use it on your own, so anything will suffice here. There's no audio, video, or templating here, so each of those radio buttons gets a "No."

The next configuration tab is the "Interaction Model." This is where you can configure the "intent model," which all custom skills require. An intent model specifies exactly which commands to detect and which surrounding words in your sentence impact them.

This single-use skill takes the shortest path through this section: type in the JSON payload seen in the first screenshot on page 156. This payload declares an intent named RecordMessage and a slot named Message. Multiuse Alexa skills require a bit more thought to set up. Under "Sample Utterances," type "RecordMessage {Message}." This tells Alexa to capture every word said after the initial "Alexa, tell bot recorder" invocation. These captured words are to be passed along as the message body for the recorder backend.

On the "Configuration" tab (shown in the second screenshot on page 156), tell Amazon that you're using your own HTTPS-enabled site to power this skill's backend. (I used a Heroku-hosted Lita bot here, so I pasted in that bot's Heroku URL with a new /alexa/recorder route tacked on to the end.) When your Lita recorder skill is built and your bot's redeployed, you'll be accepting POST requests at that URL, so be sure to plug in your app's production URL.

interaction model and creating dialog prompts

Launch Skill Builder BETA

Interaction Model ✓
Configuration ✓
SSL Certificate ✓
Test ✓
Publishing Information
Privacy & Compliance ✓

Skills Beta Testing
Status: Not yet eligible ⓘ

Intent Schema

The schema of your intents in JSON format. For more information, see Intent Schema.
You can use built-in slots and built-in intents.

```
{
  "intents": [
    {
      "slots": [
        {
          "name": "Message",
          "type": "MESSAGE"
        }
      ],
      "intent": "RecordMessage"
    }
```

Custom Slot Types

Custom you need to be referenced in the Intent Schema and Sample Utterances. For general information about custom slots, see Custom Slot Types.

Type	Values		
MESSAGE	tell my family I love them | hi mum | don't forget to turn off	Delete	Edit

Add Slot Type

Sample Utterances

These are phrases that a user is matched with your skill. Type in phrases that a user would phrase the intents. Learn more

Each of these will be used for Example Phrases, whenever that is done.

```
  RecordMessage {Message}
```

Skill Information ✓
Interaction Model ✓
Configuration ✓
SSL Certificate ✓
Test ✓
Publishing Information
Privacy & Compliance ✓

Skills Beta Testing
Status: Not yet eligible ⓘ

Global Fields

These fields apply to all languages supported by the skill.

Endpoint

Service Endpoint Type:　　　　○ AWS Lambda ARN (Amazon Resource Name) ⓘ　　　● HTTPS
　　　　　　　　　　　　　　　　　Recommended
　　　　　　　　　　　　　　　　　AWS Lambda is a server-less compute service that runs
　　　　　　　　　　　　　　　　　your code in response to events and automatically
　　　　　　　　　　　　　　　　　manages the underlying compute resources for you.
　　　　　　　　　　　　　　　　　More info about AWS Lambda
　　　　　　　　　　　　　　　　　How to integrate AWS Lambda with Alexa

Default　　　　　　　　　　　　　https://desolate-temple-13621.herokuapp.com/alexa/recorder

Provide geographical region endpoints?　　○ Yes ● No
(Follow us) ⓘ

Account Linking

Do you allow users to create an account or
link to an existing account with you?　　○ Yes ● No
Learn more

Permissions

Request users to access resources and　　☐ Device Address
capabilities
Please request permission to access user data　　　○ Full Address ⓘ
capabilities that are absolutely required as the individual　　　○ Country & Postal Code Only ⓘ
capabilities reviewed by the skill.
　　　　　　　　　　　　　　　　☐ Lists Read ⓘ

　　　　　　　　　　　　　　　　☐ Lists Write ⓘ

Alexa requires SSL-secured endpoints for custom skills. On the SSL tab shown in the following screenshot, select "My development domain is a sub-domain of a domain that has a wildcard certificate." Heroku provides these wildcard certificates automatically on their herokuapp.com domains.

On the "Test" tab, set the slider to "Enabled" so your Echo devices can talk to your new skill. Once you're done, open the Alexa app on your phone (or the web version[7]) and add the newly published skill to your personal Alexa account. You'll find it under Skills -> Your Skills.

All that's left to do now is to build the Lita backend that powers this bot recorder skill. Alexa's Service Simulator can help you generate sample inputs for your Lita skill.

Back on the Test tab (shown in the screenshot on page 158), scroll down to "Service Simulator" and type your first message, like "hello world!" Click "Ask Post to Lita-hosted Flash Briefing Feed," and you'll see an auto-generated JSON payload pop up on the left pane and a failure message in the right pane.

Excellent. You can now build a Lita route handler to receive that JSON payload, parse it, store the message in Redis, and reply with a success message.

---

7. http://alexa.amazon.com/spa/index.html#settings

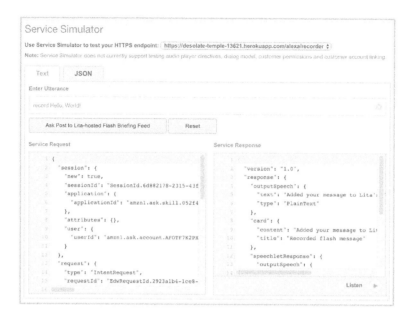

Build Out a Lita Skill to Take in Messages from Alexa

Alexa is sending you the JSON payload you need to push a user's dictated message into Lita's Redis storage. Here's a step-by-step plan to make it work:

- Tell Lita to listen for POSTs on a specific URL route.
- Route those posts to a method that parses the JSON as a Ruby hashmap.
- Extract the message you want from the hashmap.
- Pass that message on to another Lita handler using a named trigger.
- Acknowledge receipt of the message back to Alexa.

If you get stuck in implementing this Lita handler, check out my finished code on GitHub.[8] It includes all of the methods and tests described in this chapter.

Tell Lita to listen for POSTs on a specific URL route

Listening for a POST on a specific URL is a one-liner in Lita. http.post registers the handler. The first argument is the URL to listen on, and the second argument is the Ruby handler method that will receive the POST details.

lita-alexa-news-recorder/lib/lita/handlers/alexa_news_recorder.rb
```
http.post '/alexa/recorder', :record_message
```

---

8.   https://github.com/dpritchett/lita-alexa-news-recorder

Testing an HTTP handler in Lita is another one-liner. Lita is expected to route an HTTP request using method POST on route /alexa/recorder to your to-be-created :record_message method.

```
lita-alexa-news-recorder/spec/lita/handlers/alexa_news_recorder_spec.rb
describe 'routes' do
  it {
    is_expected.to route_http(:post, '/alexa/recorder')
      .to(:record_message)
  }
end
```

Route POSTs to a method that parses the JSON as Ruby hashmap

Next is the record_message handler method. This has three distinct parts.

- Extract the message from the incoming JSON payload.

- Pass the extracted message along to another Lita handler by invocation of a named Lita trigger.

- Write a JSON-formatted acknowledgment message back to the HTTP client that sent you the original message.

The extraction of the message content is handled by a separate method :extract_message, which you'll implement shortly. Note that the Rack::Request object bearing your incoming POST keeps the raw message under request.body, and you'll cast it to a plain string with request.body.string.

The intra-skill Lita trigger mechanism allows you to invoke a method on another Lita skill in the parent robot. In this case, you send robot.trigger :save_alexa_message to pass the remaining parameters along to the flash briefing skill you wrote in the previous chapter.

Finally, the client's HTTP request is acknowledged by sending back a JSON formatted string over response.write.

```
lita-alexa-news-recorder/lib/lita/handlers/alexa_news_recorder.rb
# Rack::Request, Rack::Response
def record_message(request, response)
  Lita.logger.debug(request)
  Lita.logger.debug(request.body.string)

  message = extract_message(request.body.string)
```

```
  robot.trigger(
    :save_alexa_message,
    username: 'Alexa News Recorder',
    message: message
  )

  response.write JSON.dump(alexa_response(message))
end
```

Take a high-level approach to testing :record_message. Read in a known-good Amazon JSON payload from a fixture, POST it to your Lita skill, and verify that your bot acknowledges with another properly formatted JSON string that contains the original message. You'll also want to wire up a test to verify that Lita sent the :save_alexa_message trigger out for another handler to pick up.

lita-alexa-news-recorder/spec/lita/handlers/alexa_news_recorder_spec.rb
```
describe ':record_message' do
  # "hello, Alexa" fixture
  let(:amazon_formatted_json_request_body) {
    open('./spec/fixtures/inbound_message.json').read
  }

  it 'can accept an inbound message in alexa dictation format' do
    response = http.post(
      '/alexa/recorder',
      amazon_formatted_json_request_body
    )
    body = JSON.parse(response.body, symbolize_names: true)

    expect(body.dig(:response, :outputSpeech, :text)).to include('hi dad')
  end

  it 'emits an event to trigger another handler to save alexa messages' do
    expect(robot).to receive(:trigger)
      .with(
        :save_alexa_message,
        username: 'Alexa News Recorder', message: 'hi dad'
      )

    http.post('/alexa/recorder', amazon_formatted_json_request_body)
  end
end
```

Extract the message you want from the hashmap

This extraction is an exercise in using the Ruby Hash class's :dig method to read out a specific location from within a deeply nested set of hashmaps. While the Alexa payload contains a whole pile of information, all you care about right now is what the user said after "tell bot recorder." From Alexa's perspective, that's the value of the "Message" slot under the intent communicated in the user's request.

Since third-party APIs can change without notice, throw an ArgumentError if Alexa stops sending a payload that matches the expected shape.

This method doesn't get its own unit test, because it's implicitly tested in the :record_message exercise above. That, and it respects precisely one payload shape—ArgumentErrors on failure are enough for now.

lita-alexa-news-recorder/lib/lita/handlers/alexa_news_recorder.rb
```ruby
def extract_message(payload)
  parsed = JSON.parse(payload)

  value = parsed.dig('request', 'intent', 'slots', 'Message', 'value')

  raise ArgumentError if value.nil?
  value
end
```

Acknowledge receipt of the message to Alexa

Here's an :alexa_response method that enables the main :record_message code to offload the job of converting your user's single-line, plain-text news item into a format that Alexa's web services will accept. There's not a ton to see here other than the fact that the Alexa API appears to be versioned, and the response card could be a more complicated type than a plain-text acknowledgment.

lita-alexa-news-recorder/lib/lita/handlers/alexa_news_recorder.rb
```ruby
  def alexa_response(message)
    {
      "version": "1.0",
      "sessionAttributes": {
      },
      "response": {
        "outputSpeech": {
          "type": "PlainText",
          "text": "Added your message to Lita's flash briefing: #{message}"
        },
        "card": {
          "type": "Simple",
          "title": "Recorded flash message",
          "content": "Added your message to Lita's flash briefing: #{message}"
        },
        "shouldEndSession": true
      }
    }
  end

  Lita.register_handler(self)
end
```

The test for :alexa_response is as straightforward as the method itself: Given a plain-text message, assert that the response is a deeply nested hash with the expected acknowledgment text in the expected location.

lita-alexa-news-recorder/spec/lita/handlers/alexa_news_recorder_spec.rb
```
describe ':alexa_response' do
  let(:body) { 'responding to alexa' }

  it 'should return an alexa-shaped hash with the supplied message body' do
    result = subject.alexa_response(body)

    expect(result.dig(:response, :outputSpeech, :text)).to include(body)
  end
end
```

Test recorder skill

That's it for the Alexa recorder skill. I published mine to Heroku, pointed Alexa's skill configuration at the Heroku HTTPS URL, and spoke into the Echosim tester. To test your skill after it's wired up, say this to your Echo device or Echosim:

"Alexa, tell bot recorder, 'Hello there!'"

If everything's hooked up correctly, you get an acknowledgment from the device. Check your companion newsfeed to verify that the message shows up:

You can review your Alexa interactions with the companion Alexa app as shown in the figure on page 163 or with the web-based version.[9] The Alexa app logs interactions for you to review any time.

Wrap-up

In this chapter, you built the two basic types of Alexa skills: the newsfeed and the custom skill. While these two skills work together, there's no reason you can't build standalone skills whenever you want.

---

9. https://developer.amazon.com/public/solutions/alexa/alexa-skills-kit/docs/alexa-skills-kit-interaction-model-reference#built-in-intent-library-documentation

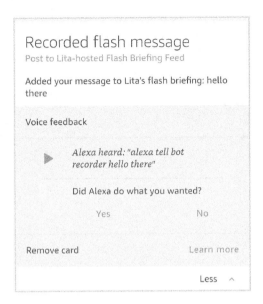

This chapter, in particular, reinforces a fundamental truth of voice assistants: you as a programmer can usually delegate the text-to-speech input and voice recognition to other software and focus on delivering simple text-first interactions for multiple platforms. You're now ready to build your own home voice assistant integrations for Alexa or other toolkits like Siri or Google Home. If you'd like, there's an Alexa marketplace where you can publish your skills to a broad audience and even charge for their use.

In the next chapter, you'll integrate Philip's Hue programmable home lighting system with your own Lita bot. From that exercise, you'll have another tool for bridging the gap between home automation and your do-everything chatbot.

Challenges

- Alexa skills can have more than one intent. Read up on them[10] and add a second interaction to your custom skill.

- The messages that Alexa records for you could go anywhere, not just back into your flash briefing. Try connecting this inbound message with one of the other messaging skills from another chapter. Send a text message, maybe an email?

- Build up an Alexa custom skill that's generalized enough to be useful to a broad audience and publish it on the Alexa skills marketplace.

---

10. https://developer.amazon.com/public/solutions/alexa/alexa-skills-kit/docs/alexa-skills-kit-interaction-model-reference#built-in-intent-library-documentation

## CHAPTER 14

Hue Programmable Lighting

In this chapter, you connect and control a set of Philips Hue light bulbs. Using Hue's LAN-based light control API and your home network, you'll turn these lights on and off and change their color—all from within your chat room. To work through this chapter, you need a Hue bridge, some Hue lights, and a computer with a home network connection.

You can purchase a bridge and white-bulb-only starter kit[1] for $100, or you can get colored bulbs for slightly more. The advantage of using colored bulbs is that you can set their color to any one of the 65,535 supported colors. Parts of this chapter assume you're using colored bulbs for the Lita commands, but you can skip those sections if you don't have access to colored bulbs.

This snippet shows a demo of the Lita commands you'll write in this chapter:

```
lita-hue-lightswitch/examples/002-lita-demo.session
$ lita
Type "exit" or "quit" to end the session.
Lita > lita hue off
Turning off light!

Lita > lita hue on
Turning on light!

Lita > lita hue color red
Setting color to red

Lita > lita hue color green
Setting color to green

Lita > lita hue demo
Enjoy the light demo!
```

---

1. https://www2.meethue.com/en-us/starter-kits

A closer look reveals there are *on* and *off* commands for switching the bulb on and off, as well as a handful of *change color to x* commands, which set your bulb's color to one of the twelve named colors. There's also a *demo* command that quickly cycles through the twelve named colors to show off Lita's Hue controls.

Before you can control your Hue light system with Lita, you need to connect the system to your computer on your local network.

Connect a Hue Bridge to Your Computer

A Hue lighting system begins with a central Hue bridge—sometimes called a hub—that connects your basic home LAN to a Zigbee wireless mesh network. The hub connects wirelessly through the Zigbee mesh to one or more Hue-compatible light bulbs.

 Joe asks:

What's a Zigbee network and how does Hue use it?

Zigbee is an open standard for wireless networking designed for Internet of Things (IoT) networks. It provides inexpensive, low-powered devices the means to communicate across a mesh network without needing to be in range of a central base point. You'll find it's not as high-bandwidth as regular Wi-Fi but much simpler and cheaper to spread to the perimeter of your home.

With your Hue system's Zigbee network, you can put a base station in one corner of your house and chain a series of bulbs to the other end of the house without having to keep each bulb near the base station. As long as a device can detect one other device on the network, it's a part of the mesh, and you can control it through your Hue system.

To connect your hub, plug it into your local network using an Ethernet connection. For most home users in the U.S., the Ethernet port is on the back of your cable or DSL modem. Next, screw your Hue bulbs into the appropriate number of nearby light sockets and power up the hub. Then, use the light switches to power up the lights.

With everything plugged in and switched on, you're ready to set up the Hue app on either an Android or iOS device. Using the Hue app, you can locate the bulbs, give them names, and associate them with separate named rooms in your home. The screenshot on page 167 shows the Hue app on iOS connected to a bridge named "Philips hue."

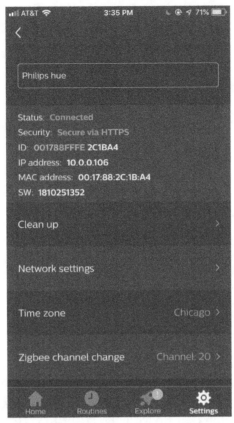

Now that you can connect to your Hue system using the Hue app, it's time to connect your hub and bulbs to Lita with a Ruby gem.

Pair your computer with the Hue bridge using the Hue gem

With your Hue bridge and computer connected to the same LAN, install the hue gem using the gem install hue command. Press the big button on top of your bridge, and start a Ruby session with pry:

```ruby
lita-hue-lightswitch/examples/001-hue-demo.rb
[1] pry(main)> require 'hue'
=> true

[2] pry(main)> client = Hue::Client.new
=> #<Hue::Client:0x0000555b194f0b40
 @bridges=
  [#<Hue::Bridge:0x0000555b194f0140
    @client=#<Hue::Client:0x0000555b194f0b40 ...>,
    @id="001788fffe2c1ba4",
    @ip="10.0.0.106">],
 @username="redacted">
```

This should work on your first try. However, if it's been more than 30 seconds since you pressed the button, you'll see a Hue::LinkButtonNotPressed error. No worries, you can press the button and run the Hue::Client.new command again. After you've successfully loaded a new Hue client object in your session, you can start playing with its API and figure out which bulbs the hub knows about and how they can be controlled. If you issue a client.lights.map(&:name) command, you'll see the names you gave your lights in the Hue mobile app:

lita-hue-lightswitch/examples/001-hue-demo.rb
```
[3] pry(main)> client.lights.map(&:name)
=> ["Bottom lamp", "Middle lamp", "Top lamp", "Bloom"]

[4] pry(main)> bloom = client.lights.last
=> #<Hue::Light:0x0000555b1970a750
 @alert="none",
 @bridge=
  #<Hue::Bridge:0x0000555b194f0140
   @client=
    #<Hue::Client:0x0000555b194f0b40
     @bridges=[#<Hue::Bridge:0x0000555b194f0140 ...>],
     @username="CSvQNKCBeyLj-FRitKTPUNRD4tEmphZIjUG1VGp1">,
   @id="001788fffe2c1ba4",
   @ip="10.0.0.106",
   @lights=
```

In this example, you can see lights named "Top lamp," "Bottom lamp," "Middle lamp," and "Bloom" (the Bloom is a model of color-changing Hue light). You should be able to match that up with your Hue app. The screenshot on page 169 from the Hue app shows a nearby Bloom model programmable color light and lists the connected light's specifications (yours will be different, of course).

Now that the hue library is connected to your bulbs, check out some of the commands in the Hue API. Use the ls command in your pry session:

lita-hue-lightswitch/examples/001-hue-demo.rb
```
[6] pry(main)> ls bloom
Hue::TranslateKeys#methods: translate_keys   unpack_hash
Hue::EditableState#methods:
  alert=         color_temperature=  hue=  on!   on?           set_xy
  brightness=    effect=                   off!  on=   saturation=
Hue::Light#methods:
  alert          color_mode          hue    name            reachable?
  bridge         color_temperature   id     name=           refresh
  brightness     effect              model  point_symbol    saturation
instance variables:
  @alert         @client        @hue     @name        @saturation
  @bridge        @color_mode    @id      @on          @software_ver
  @brightness    @effect        @model   @reachable   @state
```

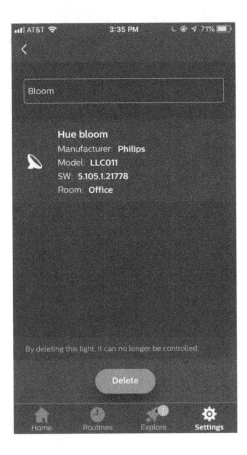

There are three commands that are useful: on!, off!, and hue=. Let's try them out one by one:

```
lita-hue-lightswitch/examples/001-hue-demo.rb
# Change my bulb to a blue color
[7] pry(main)> bloom.hue = 44444
=> 44444

# Turn off my bulb
[8] pry(main)> bloom.off!
=> false

# Turn on my bulb
[9] pry(main)> bloom.on!
=> true
```

At this point, you've written some Ruby code to connect to your Hue bridge, identify its lights, and turn them off and on. It's time to add this functionality to your Lita bot with a new handler skill.

Build a Simple Wrapper for Managing a Bulb

Begin your new skill with a call to lita handler hue-lightswitch. You get the usual Lita boilerplate structure, ready and waiting for your customizations.

Add the hue gem to your new gemspec file as in the following snippet:

lita-hue-lightswitch/lita-hue-lightswitch.gemspec
```
spec.add_runtime_dependency "lita", ">= 4.7"
spec.add_runtime_dependency "hue", "~> 0.2.0"
```

Don't forget to update the sections with TODO placeholders:

lita-hue-lightswitch/examples/003-sample.gemspec
```
spec.description   = "TODO: Add a description"
spec.summary       = "TODO: Add a summary"
spec.homepage      = "TODO: Add a homepage"
spec.license       = "TODO: Add a license"
```

With your Gemspec file built out, you can run bundle install and get to work building out your new gem, which you'll do in two phases:

- Build a Ruby class to wrap a few of the hue features in a simple package.
- Build a Lita handler class that leverages your Hue wrapper package.

Start by creating a new file named lightswitch/lib/lita/hue_colored_bulb.rb. This class wraps the low-level "enter a number between 0 and 2^16 to adjust your bulb's hue" interface into a more accessible, enter-one-of-twelve-common-color-names,-and-your-bulb-will-change-to-match"API.

Here's the basic setup of your HueColoredBulb class:

lita-hue-lightswitch/lib/lita/hue_colored_bulb.rb
```ruby
# The hue gem is doing all the heavy lifting here, you're simply
#   wrapping it in some more beginner-friendly language.
require 'hue'

# Exposes basic on, off, and recolor commands for a single named Hue bulb
#   on the local network.
class HueColoredBulb
  # Note that the initializer only cares about a single named bulb
  #   and does not look around for other bulbs to care about.
  def initialize(name='Bloom')
    @client = Hue::Client.new

    # Your client likely has multiple bulbs attached, but here you're only
    #   going to want to find a single bulb that matches the supplied name.
    @light = @client.lights.select do |light|
      light.name == name
    end.first
```

```ruby
  # No point continuing if the bulb can't be found by name.
  raise ArgumentError if @light.nil?
end

# The named light itself and the Hue client object are both worth reusing
#   as instance variables
attr_reader :light, :client
```

With the Hue bulb connection in place, you can key in the top-level methods to turn your bulb on and off and cycle through the twelve colors in a simple but catchy demo:

lita-hue-lightswitch/lib/lita/hue_colored_bulb.rb
```ruby
# on! and off! methods are passed right through this API. They're plenty
#   simple for your purposes as is.
def on!
  light.on!
end

def off!
  light.off!
end

# Fun demo to spin through all named colors, one color every quarter second.
def demo(sleep_seconds=0.25)
  colors.each do |color_name|
    self.set_color color_name
    sleep sleep_seconds
  end
end
```

The demo method leverages two undefined methods: colors and set_color. You'll build those out next. colors sketches out a twelve-color array to represent an RGB color wheel. You'll use arithmetic to associate each of these twelve named colors with a specific position on a 65,535-point RGB color wheel. set_color looks up the corresponding numeric value for a named color (for example, "red" = 0) and then sets your light's hue to match with a call to its hue= method:

lita-hue-lightswitch/lib/lita/hue_colored_bulb.rb
```ruby
# Hue's color coordinate system has about 64,000 distinct hues. For Lita
#   purposes you're fine starting with these twelve familiar options.
#
# The colors are listed in ascending order of hue along the color wheel
#   starting at red, moving clockwise up through green and blue,
#   and looping back around to the starting point to end at the same
#   red where they began.

# Each color's corresponding hue number is one-twelfth of the circle's
#   circumference higher than the previous color. If red is 0 then orange is
#   65535 / 12 * 1, or 5461. Yellow is twice that at 10,922. Rose is 60,073.
```

```ruby
#                              [R]ed
#              rose            orange
#          magenta                     yellow
#       violet                          chartreuse
#          [B]lue                    [G]reen
#                 azure         aquamarine
#                       cyan
#
def colors
  [
    'red', 'orange', 'yellow',          # red is 0
    'chartreuse', 'green', 'aquamarine', # green is 21,000
    'cyan', 'azure', 'blue',            # blue is 44,000
    'violet', 'magenta', 'rose'         # rose is about 60,000
  ]
end

# Take a color name like cyan, look up its hue on the 65000 point scale,
#    and pass that number to the light's hue= method to recolor the light.
def set_color(name)
  unless colors.include? name.downcase
    raise ArgumentError.new("I don't know that color!")
  end

  light.hue = hue_for_color(name)
end
```

The following image shows a Hue Bloom bulb in red, green, and blue. These color points are at 0, 21,845, and 43,690 on Hue's color wheel.

The next code listing implements the arithmetic required to convert a named color into its corresponding integer value on the 65,535-point RGB scale. This method saves you from having to hardcode your own integer color range limits, so it's just as effective in a 3-color system or a 24-color system:

```
lita-hue-lightswitch/lib/lita/hue_colored_bulb.rb
# RGB color wheel from 0 to 65535:
#    red is 0 (and 65535 because the wheel starts over at the end)
#    green is ~21000
#    blue is ~44000
def hue_for_color(name)
  # green has an index of 4 in the colors array above
  color_index = colors.find_index(name)

  # each color is 65535 / 12 points "wide",
  #    which is 5461 points on this RGB color wheel.
  color_width = (max_color / colors.count).to_i

  # green's hue is thus 4 * 5461 = 21845.
  color_index * color_width
end

private
# The hue gem has a built-in constant range to track the number of distinct
#    color hues the system exposes for a given colored bulb, i.e. 2^16 or
#    "16-bit" color.
def max_color
  # 0..65535
  Hue::Light::HUE_RANGE.last
end
```

That's it for the HueColoredBulb wrapper class implementation. It's time to test the wrapper.

Test your bulb control wrapper

Before you connect the bulb control wrapper to your still-empty Lita handler skill, you need to write some unit tests. Start with a new hue_colored_bulb_spec.rb file that sets the subject of your tests to a new HueColoredBulb with a specific name like "Bloom":

```
lita-hue-lightswitch/spec/lita/handlers/hue_colored_bulb_spec.rb
require "spec_helper"

describe HueColoredBulb do
  let(:bulb_name) { 'Bloom' }
  subject { described_class.new(bulb_name) }
```

With a defined subject pointing to a HueColoredBulb, you can run through a few simple tests:

```
lita-hue-lightswitch/spec/lita/handlers/hue_colored_bulb_spec.rb
it 'can turn on and off' do
  subject.on!
  subject.off!
end
```

```ruby
it 'has a list of colors' do
  actual = subject.colors
  expect(actual.first).to eq('red')
  expect(actual).to include('azure')
end

context 'setting a color' do
  it 'can be colored cyan' do
    expect{subject.set_color 'cyan'}.to_not raise_error
  end

  it 'cannot be colored burnt sienna' do
    expect{subject.set_color 'burnt_sienna'}.to raise_error(ArgumentError)
  end
end
end
```

With these tests, you can:

- Verify that you can turn the bulb on without throwing an exception.
- Turn the bulb off.
- Set the bulb to a color named "Cyan."
- Throw and catch an error with rspec when attempting to set the bulb to an unexpected color like Burnt Sienna.

The next set of tests validates the arithmetic that connects your twelve-name color wheel with the 0–65535 scale exposed by the Hue API. Your colored bulb wrapper class should know about colors of red at a hue of 0, green at ~21,000, and blue at ~44,000:

lita-hue-lightswitch/spec/lita/handlers/hue_colored_bulb_spec.rb
```ruby
context 'color hue estimations' do
  it 'has red at 0 hue' do
    actual = subject.hue_for_color 'red'
    expect(actual).to eq(0)
  end

  it 'has green at approximately 21k hue' do
    actual = subject.hue_for_color 'green'
    # absolute value of hue_for_color('green') should be within 1000
    # of the 21,000 approximation specified here.
    delta = (actual - 21000).abs
    expect(delta < 1000).to be_truthy
  end

  it 'has blue at approximately 44k hue' do
    actual = subject.hue_for_color 'blue'
    delta = (actual - 44000).abs
    expect(delta < 1000).to be_truthy
  end
end
```

This last test for your colored bulb wrapper class naively confirms that the :demo method calls :hue= only once for each color. In this case, you're looking for twelve calls to :hue= for a single call to :demo:

lita-hue-lightswitch/spec/lita/handlers/hue_colored_bulb_spec.rb
```ruby
context 'color wheel demo' do
  it 'displays each color exactly once' do
    n = subject.colors.count
    expect(subject.light).to receive(:hue=).exactly(n).times
    subject.demo(0.0001)
  end
end
```

Control Your Bulbs from Lita

You're finally ready to control your bulbs using Lita. Open the auto-generated hue_lightswitch.rb file. You'll fill this in with chat routes and handler methods that call out to the HueColoredBulb class. But first, you need to set up a :hue_bulb_name configuration variable so Lita end users can tell this skill the name of the local bulb they want to control through chat. You also need a :light method that serves as a reusable handle to a HueColoredBulb object with a connection to the specified named bulb:

lita-hue-lightswitch/lib/lita/handlers/hue_lightswitch.rb
```ruby
module Lita
  module Handlers
    class HueLightswitch < Handler

      # Set these in your bot's lita_config.rb
      config :hue_bulb_name, default: 'Bloom'

      # Create a reusable instance variable handle to a bulb
      #   named 'Bloom' (or whatever your config value for
      #   :hue_bulb_name is set to.
      def light
        @light ||= HueColoredBulb.new(config.hue_bulb_name)
      end
```

Your :light object isn't accessible to chatroom visitors until Lita has a chat route wired up to it. Type up the following call to :route and follow it with a :handle_hue method:

lita-hue-lightswitch/lib/lita/handlers/hue_lightswitch.rb
```ruby
# Any command of the form 'lita hue ____' should be caught
#   and passed to the :handle_hue method
route /^hue\s+(.+)/i, :handle_hue, command: true

# Split the captured hue command into a one-word command name
#   and everything after that (if anything) and pass the results
#   on to the :hue_execute mapping below.
```

```ruby
def handle_hue(message)
  command, *rest = message.matches.last.last.split
  response = hue_execute(command, rest)
  message.reply response
end
```

Next, you need to work on the execute method. The :hue_execute method demonstrates a way of hiding a multi-directional command evaluation process behind a single Lita route. While this method was written to respond differently based completely on the contents of the supplied command parameter, you could also choose to write separate Lita routes for each of these actions. The else case prints out a basic I-don't-know-what-to-do response for unexpected commands like "lita hue do a barrel roll."

lita-hue-lightswitch/lib/lita/handlers/hue_lightswitch.rb
```ruby
# Given a one-word hue :command and a possibly-empty array of
#    additional parameters :rest, step through this case
#    statement and perform the first matching action.
def hue_execute(command, rest=[])
  case command
  when 'demo'
    demo
    'Enjoy the light demo!'
  when 'list_colors'
    list_colors
  when 'color'
    recolor rest
    "Setting color to #{rest.join ' '}"
  when 'off'
    off!
    "Turning off light!"
  when 'on'
    on!
    "Turning on light!"
  else
    debug_message = [command, rest].flatten.join ' '
    "I don't know how to [#{debug_message}] a hue bulb."
  end
end
```

The regular expression in the route is filtered through the handler method like this:

- User sends a message that looks like "lita hue color green."

- Lita's route matches "hue color green" and passes it to the :handle_hue method.

- handle_hue splits the "hue color green" into a command variable set to "color" and a rest array set to ["green"], and it passes both variables over to hue_execute.

- hue_execute returns a plain-text response, and Lita sends that back out to the chatroom user as a reply.

The next listing shows the list_colors method and a recolor method. list_colors is a human-friendly take on the Which-colors-does-Lita-know-the-names-of-again? question. recolor handles commands like "lita hue color blue" by passing off a corresponding :set_color to the HueColoredBulb object.

lita-hue-lightswitch/lib/lita/handlers/hue_lightswitch.rb
```ruby
# Simple help text in case someone forgets Lita's `hue` commands
def list_colors
  light.colors.join ' '
end

# Set the bulb's color to one of the named colors it recognizes
#    e.g. red, green, blue, etc.
def recolor(rest)
  new_color = rest.first
  light.set_color new_color
end
```

Finally, you need to add links to the :off!, :on!, and :demo methods you built into your HueColoredBulb class, so that chat users can explore all of the abilities you built into your colored light bulb skill:

lita-hue-lightswitch/lib/lita/handlers/hue_lightswitch.rb
```ruby
#################
#
# These three commands are pass-throughs to the HueColoredBulb wrapper.
#
#################

def off!
  light.off!
end

def on!
  light.on!
end

def demo
  light.demo
end
```

That's it for the implementation of the Hue light bulb controller skill for your Lita bot. Ready for some testing?

Test your Hue controller skill

You should have a hue_lightswitch_spec.rb file waiting for you, because you started this chapter by running lita handler hue_lightswitch. Open the file and set up the basic describe / subject header:

```
lita-hue-lightswitch/spec/lita/handlers/hue_lightswitch_spec.rb
require "spec_helper"

describe Lita::Handlers::HueLightswitch, lita_handler: true do
  subject { described_class.new(robot) }
```

Once you have a subject loading up your new Lita skill, you can start testing its functionality. Start by verifying that the skill is prepared to receive messages like "hue color green" and "hue off":

```
lita-hue-lightswitch/spec/lita/handlers/hue_lightswitch_spec.rb
it { is_expected.to route("Lita hue color green") }
it { is_expected.to route("Lita hue list_colors") }
it { is_expected.to route("Lita hue off") }
it { is_expected.to route("Lita hue on") }
```

If your skill passes the simplest of route tests, you're ready to set up a dummy object to stand in for a HueColoredBulb and pass it to your test object as a test double named :bulb. The following calls to before ensure that your test double acts enough like a HueColoredBulb to keep the test suite going:

```
lita-hue-lightswitch/spec/lita/handlers/hue_lightswitch_spec.rb
context 'using a dummy HueColoredBulb client' do
  let(:bulb) { double(:bulb) }
  before { subject.stub(:light).and_return bulb }
  # Intentionally deviating from the color list of the actual
  #   HueColoredBulb class for two reasons:
  #   - three colors make for simpler testing than 12
  #   - violating some of the numeric assumptions of the linked
  #       class might give us a more robust integration by assuming
  #       as little as necessary from this calling class.
  before { bulb.stub(:colors).and_return %w[red orange green] }
```

Your Lita skill should be able to turn its bulb on and off and to confirm those actions through chat:

```
lita-hue-lightswitch/spec/lita/handlers/hue_lightswitch_spec.rb
it 'can turn off the bulb' do
  expect(bulb).to receive(:off!)
  actual = subject.hue_execute 'off'
  expect(actual).to match /Turning off/
end
```

```
it 'can turn off the bulb' do
  expect(bulb).to receive(:on!)
  actual = subject.hue_execute 'on'
  expect(actual).to match /Turning on/
end
```

Your skill should gracefully handle list colors and color ___ commands with the expected confirmation output. In the final set of tests, validate the availability of a few common color names and confirm that Lita can apply those colors to your Hue bulb:

lita-hue-lightswitch/spec/lita/handlers/hue_lightswitch_spec.rb
```
it 'can list colors' do
  actual = subject.list_colors
  expect(actual).to include 'green'
  expect(actual).to include 'red'
  expect(actual).to include 'orange'
end

it 'can recolor the bulb' do
  new_color = bulb.colors.sample

  expect(bulb).to receive(:set_color)
  actual = subject.hue_execute "color", [new_color]
  expect(actual).to match /Setting color to #{new_color}/
end
```

Wrap-up

In this chapter, you integrated your own systems with other systems and IoT devices, which allowed you to control your Hue lights using Lita. You also saw how you could overlay a simple, user-friendly subset of functionality on top of an open-ended API (twelve colors versus 65,000). You used subtle Ruby arithmetic to provide a programmer-friendly interface to some otherwise opaque-looking mathematical functions. Last but not least, you used case statements to provide multiple functions behind a single chat route. This isn't always the best choice, but it's a good tool to have available for a simpler skill.

That was a lot of work, but you now have a good working foundation for connecting to IoT systems across your home LAN.

Challenges

- Update this gem to handle multiple bulbs (check out the named room groupings available from the hue gem).

- Add some inspection and debugging output to your skill in case users don't know what Hue devices are connected to the system. Self-service troubleshooting is good for users and maintainers.

- Combine this skill with the task scheduler from earlier in the book to have Lita turn your lights off and on in the future. Maybe you can prank a friend.

Index

Thank you!

How did you enjoy this book? Please let us know. Take a moment to email us at support@pragprog.com with your feedback. Tell us your story and you could win free ebooks. Please use the subject "Book Feedback."

Ready for your next great Pragmatic Bookshelf book? Come on over to https://pragprog.com and use the coupon code BUYANOTHER2019 to save 30% on your next ebook.

Void where prohibited, restricted, or otherwise unwelcome. Do not use ebooks near water. If rash persists, see a doctor. Doesn't apply to *The Pragmatic Programmer* ebook, because it's older than the Pragmatic Bookshelf itself. Side effects may include increased knowledge and skill, increased marketability, and deep satisfaction. Increase dosage regularly.

And thank you for your continued support,

Andy Hunt, Publisher

SAVE 30%!
Use coupon code
BUYANOTHER2019

A Scrum Book

Gain insights and depth of rationale into Scrum from many highly respected world authorities, including one of its founders, who lead you through the deep foundations of Scrum's structure and practice. Enhance and customize your Scrum practice with ninety-four organizational building blocks, called patterns, that you can freely and flexibly choose from to fit your needs. Understand and appreciate the history of Scrum and the role it plays in solving common problems in product development.

Jeff Sutherland, James O. Coplien, and The Scrum Patterns Group
(540 pages) ISBN: 9781680506716. $59.95
https://pragprog.com/book/jcscrum

Manage Your Project Portfolio, Second Edition

You have too many projects, and firefighting and multitasking are keeping you from finishing any of them. You need to manage your project portfolio. This fully updated and expanded bestseller arms you with agile and lean ways to collect all your work and decide which projects you should do first, second, and never. See how to tie your work to your organization's mission and show your managers, your board, and your staff what you can accomplish and when. Picture the work you have, and make those difficult decisions, ensuring that all your strength is focused where it needs to be.

This new edition features a free downloadable workbook that puts you on the fast track to creating your project portfolio. Pulling together key checklists, steps, and kanbans from the book, this workbook will help you get your ideas flowing and create something tangible. You'll find the workbook here.

Johanna Rothman
(240 pages) ISBN: 9781680501759. $36
https://pragprog.com/book/jrport2

Forge Your Future with Open Source

Free and open source is the foundation of software development, and it's built by people just like you. Discover the fundamental tenets that drive the movement. Take control of your career by selecting the right project to meet your professional goals. Master the language and avoid the pitfalls that typically ensnare new contributors. Join a community of like-minded people and change the world. Programmers, writers, designers, and everyone interested in software will make their mark through free and open source software contributions.

VM (Vicky) Brasseur
(222 pages) ISBN: 9781680503012. $33.95
https://pragprog.com/book/vbopens

Fire in the Valley

In the 1970s, while their contemporaries were protesting the computer as a tool of dehumanization and oppression, a motley collection of college dropouts, hippies, and electronics fanatics were engaged in something much more subversive. Obsessed with the idea of getting computer power into their own hands, they launched from their garages a hobbyist movement that grew into an industry, and ultimately a social and technological revolution. What they did was invent the personal computer: not just a new device, but a watershed in the relationship between man and machine. This is their story.

Michael Swaine and Paul Freiberger
(422 pages) ISBN: 9781937785765. $34
https://pragprog.com/book/fsfire

The Pragmatic Bookshelf

The Pragmatic Bookshelf features books written by developers for developers. The titles continue the well-known Pragmatic Programmer style and continue to garner awards and rave reviews. As development gets more and more difficult, the Pragmatic Programmers will be there with more titles and products to help you stay on top of your game.

Visit Us Online

This Book's Home Page
https://pragprog.com/book/dpchat
Source code from this book, errata, and other resources. Come give us feedback, too!

Keep Up to Date
https://pragprog.com
Join our announcement mailing list (low volume) or follow us on twitter @pragprog for new titles, sales, coupons, hot tips, and more.

New and Noteworthy
https://pragprog.com/news
Check out the latest pragmatic developments, new titles and other offerings.

Save on the eBook

Save on the eBook versions of this title. Owning the paper version of this book entitles you to purchase the electronic versions at a terrific discount.

PDFs are great for carrying around on your laptop—they are hyperlinked, have color, and are fully searchable. Most titles are also available for the iPhone and iPod touch, Amazon Kindle, and other popular e-book readers.

Buy now at *https://pragprog.com/coupon*

Contact Us

Online Orders:	*https://pragprog.com/catalog*
Customer Service:	*support@pragprog.com*
International Rights:	*translations@pragprog.com*
Academic Use:	*academic@pragprog.com*
Write for Us:	*http://write-for-us.pragprog.com*
Or Call:	+1 800-699-7764